Breakfast in Bed

Breakfast in Bed

90 Recipes for Creative Indulgences

Jesse Ziff Cool

HarperCollins*Publishers*

For my parents,
June and Eddie Ziff, who lovingly tucked me into bed
and endlessly nurtured me through food and a
soft hand on my brow

. . . .

BREAKFAST IN BED. Copyright © 1997 by Jesse Ziff Cool. All rights reserved. No part of this book may be used or reproduced in any manner whatsoever without written permission except in the case of brief quotations embodied in critical articles and reviews. For information, address HarperCollins Publishers, Inc., 10 East 53rd Street, New York, NY 10022.

HarperCollins books may be purchased for educational, business, or sales promotional use. For information please write: Special Markets Department, HarperCollins Publishers, Inc., 10 East 53rd Street, New York, NY 10022.

FIRST EDITION

Designed by Renato Stanisic

Library of Congress Cataloging-in-Publication Data

Cool, Jesse Ziff.
    Breakfast in bed / by Jesse Ziff Cool. — 1st ed.
        p.   cm.
    Includes index.
    ISBN 0-00-225098-5
    1. Breakfasts.   I. Title.
TX733.C6834   1997
641.5'2—dc21   97-1052

98 99 00 01 ❖/HK 10 9 8 7 6 5 4 3 2

Printed in Hong Kong

ACKNOWLEDGMENTS

To my children, Joshua Danovitz and Jonah Cool, for appreciating my dedication to starting their days with hearty, homecooked breakfasts instead of handing them a box of cereal and a carton of milk.

To Meesha Halm, who accepted this book and lovingly and endlessly believes in me as a writer.

To Beth Henspberger, who is always willing to share.

To David Gorn, Eric Mason, Steve Mangold, Diane Levy, Linda Krain, Lolly Font, Kathleen Samuels, Elizabeth Fenwick, Stuart Dickson, Sara Baer-Sinnott, Len Robinson, and my brothers, David and Danny Ziff.

For genuine encouragement and support, my extraordinary staff at Flea St.

For the patience and partnership that created the images and style of this book, Noel Barnhurst and the design team in New York.

And very special thanks to Christine Gutierrez, pastry chef at Flea St., who tested the recipes and diligently caught me when needed.

CONTENTS

SPOON FOODS

PANCAKES AND WAFFLES

BAKED GOODS

SIDE ORDERS

MENU SUGGESTIONS 113

INDEX 116

BLINTZES WITH BERRIES (PAGE 15)

Introduction

Eight-fifteen on a sunny June morning. I whisper, "Don't move, I'll be right back." I return with food and coffee on a bed tray, and suddenly this Sunday morning has limitless possibilities. There is no real reason for serving my sweetheart breakfast in bed this morning, but that's the best part—creating a special day out of one that would otherwise be like any other. I keep the food simple and elegant: toast with homemade jam and sweet butter served with a bowl of fresh berries and Devon cream. I squeeze some fresh orange juice and crawl back into bed with the man I love.

The goal of this book is to seduce you into experiencing and sharing the pleasures of breakfast in bed. If you are one who cringes at the thought of crumbs on your sheets, this might not be the book for you. But if you are like me, you understand that beds are meant for much more than sleeping. I have been known to take the calculator to bed and pay bills. I wrote much of my first cookbook in bed on my laptop computer. Quite simply, my bed is my favorite place to be. With six or eight pillows, a down quilt, and cotton sheets, it beckons to me at all times of the day. It isn't necessarily about sexiness, though of course it can be. It is about softness and comfort, about stopping to nurture myself in body and spirit.

The very best way of taking care of myself is to eat in bed. There is something almost indecently delicious about the experience. Whether

I'm sharing a split of good champagne with my lover or snuggled into my flannel nightgown with a takeout carton of egg foo yung watching an old movie on TV, I am as happy as I can be. Those feelings go back to the rare and wonderful times in my childhood when my mother would give me my meals in bed. When she plumped my pillows, smoothed my blankets, and placed a bed tray of my favorite foods on my lap, I felt as loved and as special as I ever have.

Those are the feelings I hope *Breakfast in Bed* will help you to share—with a sweetheart who needs to feel your love in a new way, with a spouse who needs strength to face a tough day, with a sick child who needs a little extra TLC, with an aging parent who needs to be reminded of her importance. To begin someone else's day with consideration and affection. To ask nothing in return. This is love. And when you care for someone else in this way, you are caring for yourself.

It takes a little time to do this, of course. But with the "Do Ahead" tips included with each recipe, your breakfast can be ready in as little as five minutes, and rarely more than thirty or forty-five minutes in the morning. And don't forget that breakfast in bed can be as simple as a cup of perfectly brewed tea or coffee, or a luscious fresh peach cut and carefully arranged on a beautiful plate.

When I began talking about this book to friends, most sighed and said they wished someone would serve them breakfast in bed. If this book is an impetus for you to start someone's day with love and care, then it is a success.

Where It Began: Late for the Train

I settled in Palo Alto, California, in 1975 after traveling across the southernmost part of the United States for two months in a 1965 Volkswagen van. My son Joshua was five, and I was a single mother. To make ends meet, I got a job waiting tables at the Good Earth Restaurant. I chose the morning-lunch shift so I could be home to tuck Joshua into bed at night and send him off to school in the early morning, and I learned to love it. There is something humbling about sharing the beginning of someone else's day, and I felt an obligation to both my child and my customers to serve breakfast with nurturing and care.

It was at the Good Earth that I met the man who was for a time my husband. He and a friend had restaurant fantasies, and we teamed up to open Late for the Train. The original location was considered a terrible one at the time—adjacent to the railroad tracks and the Menlo Park train station. The three of us put our hearts and souls into that little cinder-block building. We had a deep commitment to real food, free of artificial anything, touched by people rather than machines. That philosophy was at the core of a food style that twenty years ago was neither trendy nor fashionable, but to me was unquestionably responsible. I still think so today.

We believed in starting people's days with hearty, healthy food served in a warm and gentle environment. The tables were draped with soft peach tablecloths. Little vases of flowers and tubs of apple butter sat upon antique lace doilies. The people on the staff were personable and artistic. We wanted our customers to think of themselves as guests.

It was a magical restaurant, and the morning hours were the best of all. When the doors opened at 7 A.M., soft music met people as they crossed the threshold. A cup of coffee or tea was placed before them as quickly as possible. On busy days, we passed a tray of fresh strawberries to those waiting for a table.

I learned that breakfast is a time when you can make a small difference in someone's life, that the physical and emotional nourishment you give them are something they can carry with them the rest of the day.

Where It Began: The Lilac House

When I walk each morning in the foothills of the Santa Cruz Mountains, my path goes past a little spot that reminds me of a special hiding place I had as a child. At the back of a neighbor's big backyard, bordering acres of pastures, was an overgrown clump of lilac bushes that formed a cavelike hideaway. It became a magical playhouse where I established a domain with makeshift benches, tables, and anything else my mom would give me for those pretend hours as a schoolteacher, nurse, housekeeper, cook, or waitress.

Sometimes my brothers spent the night in the cozy little lilac house, and I would appear in the morning with a simple breakfast. They had to be nice to me because they were in my space and, more important, they wanted the food. In order to get it, they had to join me in my fantasy world. We sat on little tables covered with old cloths, ate from doll-sized plates, and drank juice from tiny teacups.

Today when I walk past the cavernous little spot on my daily workout, I want to find some old crates and benches, sit down to breakfast with some little person, and tell about the sweet, simple life beneath those lilac bushes.

Fruit

The simple act of serving a bowl of perfect berries or half a sweet grapefruit broiled for a moment or two can be enough to please any bed partner. A melon garnished with fresh mint leaves and served with thick slices of earthy whole grain toast is a marvelous way to begin the day, too. Fresh, succulent figs with raspberries and goat cheese are paradise in my mouth. And there are times when wedges of sweet oranges, peaches, or apples from your own yard or the farmer's market are as good as it gets.

But the purpose of this book is to discover sensual treats to serve to others or yourself to make the beginning of the day special. With a little effort, that piece of fruit can be transformed into something glorious. A plate of berries and sliced fruit garnished with edible flowers and sprigs of herbs, for example, can be taken a step further with a bit of goat cheese or salty prosciutto or smoked chicken.

The most important thing to remember about serving fruit for breakfast is to pay attention to the seasons. Summer is the time to eat a wide variety of naturally ripened fruit. In fall and winter, pears, apples, or dried fruit can be deeply nurturing. I don't want to eat raspberries in the middle of winter even if they are offered at many grocery stores. I would rather get creative and warm up my house with an apple dumpling or a dried fruit pizza baking in the oven.

Quick Fruit Butters

At my restaurant, Flea St., we make fresh seasonal fruit butters every week to serve at Sunday brunch with our warm buttermilk biscuits. The butters are a big hit because they are not loaded with sugar and can be spread thickly over the fluffy biscuits. They're great with smoked sausages and other meats, too.

Fruit butters are embarrassingly easy to make. I don't take the time to seal them for long storage because we eat them so quickly. They can be made ahead of time and stored in the refrigerator for at least a week. Serve them chilled or warm them slightly in a saucepan or in the microwave for a fresher, more homemade flavor.

APPLE OR PEAR BUTTER

Makes about 3 cups

2 POUNDS COOKING APPLES OR PEARS, PEELED AND CORED
1 CINNAMON STICK
1 CUP BROWN SUGAR
GRATED ZEST OF 1 LEMON
½ TEASPOON GROUND CLOVES
APPLE JUICE

In a heavy saucepan, combine the fruit, cinnamon stick, brown sugar, lemon zest, and cloves. Add enough apple juice just to cover, and bring it to a simmer. Cook, uncovered, until the fruit is soft, 15 to 30 minutes. Strain off any excess juices and remove the cinnamon stick. Mash by hand for a chunky butter or in a food processor for a smooth butter.

DRIED APRICOT OR FIG BUTTER

Makes about 3 cups

1 POUND DRIED FIGS OR UNSULFURED APRICOTS
1½ CUPS ORANGE JUICE
1 WHOLE VANILLA BEAN

Pick or cut off any stems on figs. Combine the dried fruit, orange juice, and vanilla bean in a heavy saucepan. Bring the mixture to a simmer and cook, covered, until fruit has softened, about 5 minutes. Drain off excess juice and puree in a food processor or blender.

FRESH PEACH BUTTER

Makes about 2 cups

1½ POUNDS RIPE PEACHES
½ CUP BROWN SUGAR
½ VANILLA BEAN
½ TEASPOON GROUND CLOVES

Bring a large pot of water to a boil. Drop the peaches in the water until the skin loosens, 1 to 3 minutes (the riper the peaches the less time it takes). Put the peaches in a bowl of ice water and peel off the skins. Remove the pits.

Put the peach flesh in a heavy saucepan with the sugar, vanilla bean, and cloves. Bring to a simmer over low heat and cook, covered, for about 10 minutes, until the peaches are soft. Remove the vanilla bean. Mash the fruit by hand for chunky butter or puree in a food processor for a smooth butter.

FRESH BERRY BUTTER

Use strawberries, blackberries, blueberries, loganberries, or just about any berry.

Makes about 1½ cups

2 PINTS FRESH BERRIES
¼ CUP SUGAR PLUS MORE TO TASTE
1 TABLESPOON FINELY GRATED ORANGE ZEST
2 TABLESPOONS GRAND MARNIER (OPTIONAL)

Wash the berries and remove any stems. Put them in a heavy saucepan with about ¼ cup sugar. Bring to a simmer and cook, uncovered, until the berries are soft, about 20 minutes. Taste for sweetness and add more sugar if needed. If the fruit is very watery, strain off some of the juice. Cool and stir in the orange zest and Grand Marnier.

FRESH BERRIES WITH CRÈME FRAÎCHE

The traditional way to prepare crème fraîche is with buttermilk, but Julia Child discovered years ago that blending sour cream with heavy cream produces the same results. In a pinch, commercially prepared crème fraîche is available in the dairy case of most well-stocked grocery stores.

2 servings, with leftover crème fraîche

2 CUPS HEAVY CREAM
½ CUP SOUR CREAM
1 PINT STRAWBERRIES, RASPBERRIES, OR OTHER FRESH BERRIES

Stir the heavy cream and sour cream together in a saucepan. Heat it over medium heat just until it's slightly warm to the touch (about 90 degrees), about 3 minutes.

Pour the mixture into a clean ceramic bowl, cover it with a cloth, and put it in a warm spot—a place where you would put bread dough to rise—for about 8 hours. Refrigerate it overnight. The thickening will continue as it cools, and the crème will be ready to eat in the morning. It will keep in the refrigerator for several weeks.

Wash the berries, slice them if needed, and serve them with generous dollops of crème fraîche.

. . . .

Do Ahead: Make the crème fraîche and wash the berries.

In the Morning (about 5 minutes): Slice the berries if needed and top with crème fraîche.

. . . .

BAGUETTE WITH CAMBOZOLA BRIE, CHIVES, AND STRAWBERRIES

The marriage of the blue brie and luscious ripe strawberries is not only a memorable taste experience but a feast for the eye. A glass of fresh orange juice or Grenache or a bowl of sliced peaches flecked with fresh mint can make this breakfast unspeakably sensual.

2 to 4 servings

1 SWEET BAGUETTE

5 OR 6 FRESH STRAWBERRIES

6 TO 8 OUNCES CAMBOZOLA OR SAGA BLUE BRIE, AT ROOM TEMPERATURE

¼ CUP CHOPPED FRESH CHIVES

CHIVE BLOSSOMS FOR GARNISH (OPTIONAL)

Preheat the oven or toaster oven to 350 degrees and warm the baguette for 5 minutes. Meanwhile, wash, dry, hull, and slice the strawberries.

Remove the bread from the oven and cut it at an angle into ¾-inch slices. Spread each slice generously with cheese and sprinkle with chives. Arrange strawberry slices on top, and garnish with chive blossoms.

. . . .

Do Ahead: Soften cheese at room temperature overnight. Hull, wash, and dry the berries and chop the chives; refrigerate, covered.

In the Morning (about 10 minutes): Warm and slice the bread, slice the strawberries, and assemble.

. . . .

PEACHES IN BASIL AND BALSAMIC VINEGAR WITH BAGUETTE AND CHIVE-GERANIUM CREAM CHEESE

Choose firm, ripe peaches, freestone if possible. Treat yourself to a well-aged bottle of balsamic vinegar; you get what you pay for. Use only unsprayed, organic geraniums picked from your garden. If you don't grow geraniums, substitute rose petals or pansy petals. Buy an unsliced loaf of bread so you can hand-slice it thickly. And take the simplicity of bread, fruit, and cheese and transform it into a feast.

2 servings, with leftovers

2 OR 3 RIPE PEACHES, PEELED, PITTED, AND SLICED

½ TEASPOON BALSAMIC VINEGAR PLUS MORE TO TASTE

3 OR 4 LARGE PURPLE OR GREEN BASIL LEAVES, CHOPPED

4 OUNCES CREAM CHEESE, SOFTENED

1 TABLESPOON CHOPPED CHIVES

2 TABLESPOONS CHOPPED GERANIUM PETALS

PINCH OF CAYENNE (OPTIONAL)

1 SWEET BAGUETTE, CUT INTO ¾-INCH-THICK SLICES

BASIL LEAVES AND GERANIUM BLOSSOMS FOR GARNISH (OPTIONAL)

In a small bowl, toss the peaches with ½ teaspoon balsamic vinegar and the chopped basil. Add more vinegar to taste. Place the bowl in the center of a medium plate.

In another small bowl, thoroughly blend the cream cheese with the chives and chopped geranium petals. Season with cayenne if you choose.

Generously spread the baguette slices with the cream cheese mixture, and arrange them on the plate around the peaches. Garnish with basil leaves and geranium blossoms if you like.

....

DO AHEAD: Blend the cream cheese mixture. Refrigerate, covered.

IN THE MORNING (ABOUT 15 MINUTES): Take the cheese out 10 or 15 minutes before serving to soften. Peel, pit, and slice the peaches and toss with the vinegar and basil. Slice the baguette, spread it with the cream cheese mixture, and arrange with peaches on a plate.

....

MELON WITH PROSCIUTTO, MINT, AND CHAMPAGNE

In the heat of the summer, nothing compares to fresh melon, juicy, ripe, and dripping with perfume. The sweetness is heightened by a thin wrap of proscuitto and glorified with a hint of fresh mint. A fresh baguette and sweet butter are the perfect accompaniment.

Go to a good deli for the prosciutto. Ask the clerk to slice it paper-thin, and place it carefully in the wrapping paper so that you'll be able to separate the tender slices without tearing them.

Buy the best champagne or sparkling wine you can afford; a cheap bottle can be a ticket for a mid-morning headache. Splash some over the melon just before serving, fill the flutes, and head back to bed. Drinking champagne with a sweetheart under the covers is almost as luscious as the melon itself.

2 servings

1 MEDIUM MELON (CANTALOUPE,
    HONEYDEW, CRENSHAW, OR CASABA)
6 TO 8 MINT LEAVES
2 OUNCES LEAN PROSCIUTTO,
    SLICED THIN
1 TABLESPOON CAPERS FOR GARNISH
    (OPTIONAL)
FRESHLY GROUND PEPPER FOR GARNISH
    (OPTIONAL)
1 BOTTLE TOP-QUALITY CHAMPAGNE OR OTHER
    SPARKLING WINE, CHILLED (SEE NOTE)

With a sharp knife, peel the whole melon. Cut it in half, and scrape out and discard the seeds. Cut the flesh lengthwise into ¾-inch-thick slices. (If you find it easier to peel the melon after it's sliced, that's fine, too.)

Chop the mint, reserving a few leaves for garnish.

Carefully wrap a piece of prosciutto around the middle of each melon wedge. Arrange the slices on one large plate or two smaller ones. Garnish with mint and, if you like, capers and pepper.

Open the champagne and drizzle about 2 tablespoons over the melon. Pour more champagne into two flutes. Serve immediately.

NOTE: Use a split or 350 ml bottle for about 1½ glasses of champagne per person, a full 750 ml bottle for about 2½ glasses per person.

. . . .

DO AHEAD: Peel, halve, and seed the melon, and refrigerate it, tightly wrapped.

IN THE MORNING (10 MINUTES): Slice the melon, chop the mint, and assemble the dish.

. . . .

Warm Poached Figs in Cinnamon Anise Hyssop Broth with Fresh Raspberries

Figs are one of the most sensual fruits that have ever touched my lips. I like them best when they are very ripe, shriveled, and beginning to dry, full of natural sugars. Both raspberries and figs are available in late summer, and the combination is extraordinary.

Anise hyssop is an heirloom herb that has the essence of anise and mint. The delicate lavender blossoms are beautiful as a garnish or served in a vase next to the figs. If you can't find anise hyssop, use a combination of fresh mint and fennel tops.

Serve this dish with thick slices of warm or toasted whole grain bread for a healthy yet seductive breakfast.

2 servings

2 CUPS APPLE JUICE

JUICE OF 1 LARGE LEMON

1 CINNAMON STICK, BROKEN

3 WHOLE CLOVES

3 ANISE HYSSOP LEAVES OR A LARGE SPEARMINT LEAF OR A SMALL HANDFUL OF FENNEL TOPS

6 VERY RIPE FRESH FIGS

½ PINT RED OR BLACK RASPBERRIES

ANISE HYSSOP BLOSSOMS OR FENNEL TOPS FOR GARNISH

Combine the apple juice, lemon juice, cinnamon, cloves, and the anise hyssop leaves in a saucepan and bring to a simmer over medium-low heat. Cook, uncovered, for 10 minutes, reducing liquid by one-third. Add the figs and simmer, covered, 10 minutes longer, or until the figs are very soft.

With a slotted spoon, remove the figs to two individual bowls. Strain the juice, return it to the pan, and reduce it by half over high heat, until it becomes somewhat syrupy. Top the figs with the raspberries and anise hyssop blossoms, and drizzle a little of the reduced juice over all.

· ·

DO AHEAD: The figs can be cooked up to a few days in advance, refrigerated in their cooking liquid, and warmed when ready to serve.

IN THE MORNING (10 MINUTES OR LESS): Warm the figs, reduce the liquid, prepare the garnish, and assemble the dish.

· ·

MAPLE-BAKED PEARS WITH AGED CHEDDAR

On a cold winter morning when the last thing you want to do is get out of bed, a dish of warm pears and salty cheese might help you muster just enough energy to sit up and read a book or watch a morning movie on TV. These pears are wonderful with crusty bread and steaming hot cups of Darjeeling tea laced with milk and sugar.

4 servings

4 FIRM RIPE PEARS

2 CUPS WATER

½ CUP MAPLE SYRUP

½ CUP WHITE RAISINS

1 TEASPOON GROUND CINNAMON

1 TEASPOON GROUND ALLSPICE

2 TABLESPOONS BRANDY

4 OUNCES SHARP CHEDDAR CHEESE, BROKEN INTO SMALL BITS

MINT LEAVES FOR GARNISH (OPTIONAL)

Preheat the oven to 375 degrees. Peel the pears, cut them in half, and remove the seeds. Place them cut side up in a deep baking dish.

In a saucepan, combine the water, maple syrup, raisins, cinnamon, allspice, and brandy. Bring the liquid to a boil, reduce the heat to low, and simmer for 10 minutes to thicken slightly. Pour the sauce over the pears, turning them to completely coat.

Bake the pears for about 30 minutes, until soft in the center, basting them every 10 minutes with the sauce. Set them aside to cool slightly.

To serve, ladle a few tablespoons of sauce into each shallow bowl. Sprinkle bits of cheese on top of the sauce. Place two pear halves in each bowl, and drizzle with a bit more sauce. Garnish with mint if you like, and serve immediately.

. . . .

DO AHEAD: Bake the pears; break the cheese into small pieces. Refrigerate separately, tightly covered.

IN THE MORNING (20 MINUTES): Warm the pears in a preheated, 400-degree oven for about 10 minutes. Proceed with serving instructions above.

. . . .

FRESH FRUIT OMELET

Think of this as a quick and easy fruit crepe. Choose the fruit according to the season: in summer, use berries, pitted cherries, or sliced peaches, nectarines, or apricots. In fall, try fresh figs or sliced pears, persimmons, or apples sautéed in a little butter until soft. In winter, I like tropical fruits such as sliced bananas, papaya, or pineapple.

2 servings

2 CUPS FRESH FRUIT (SEE ABOVE)

⅓ CUP SOUR CREAM OR YOGURT

2 OR 3 TABLESPOONS HONEY

½ TEASPOON GROUND CINNAMON

2 TABLESPOONS BUTTER

4 TO 6 EGGS, WELL BEATEN

3 OUNCES CHEDDAR OR GOAT CHEESE,
  GRATED OR CRUMBLED

CHOPPED FRESH MINT FOR GARNISH
  (OPTIONAL)

Position an oven rack 6 to 8 inches from the broiler, and preheat the broiler.

Clean the fruit and cut it into bite-size pieces if necessary. Set aside.

In a small bowl, stir together the sour cream, honey, and cinnamon. Set aside.

Melt half the butter in an 8- to 10-inch omelet pan or skillet over medium heat. Pour in half the beaten eggs. As the eggs cook, use a spatula to lift the edges, letting the uncooked egg run underneath. When no loose egg will move to the edge, remove the pan from the heat and sprinkle on half the cheese. Place the pan under the broiler just until the cheese is melted and the egg is completely set.

Spread half the fruit on one side of the omelet, and top it with a generous dollop of the sour cream mixture. Fold the other side over the fruit, and slide the omelet onto a plate. Garnish with more sour cream mixture and fresh mint. Cook the second omelet in the same way; that one is for you!

. . . .

DO AHEAD: Stir together the sour cream mixture. Wash the fruit; peel and cut any that won't discolor or soften; cook if desired. Crumble the cheese. Store all, covered, in the refrigerator.

IN THE MORNING (15 TO 20 MINUTES): Cook and fill the omelets as directed. Sprinkle fresh mint on top if desired.

. . . .

BLINTZES WITH BERRIES

Blintzes—cheese-stuffed crepes—are a natural for breakfast. They can be rolled a day in advance and freeze well. All you have to do is crawl out of bed in the morning, warm a little butter in a heavy pan, brown the blintzes, cut up some fruit, and crawl back into bed to eat. As a kid, I ate them smothered in sour cream with a drizzle of maple syrup—a great option when you want some kid-like nurturing or when fresh berries are out of season. When they are in season, use strawberries, blueberries, blackberries, or raspberries.

12 blintzes, 4 to 6 servings

FOR THE CREPES

¾ CUP UNBLEACHED WHITE FLOUR

¼ TEASPOON SALT

4 EGGS, BEATEN

1 CUP MILK

3 TABLESPOONS BUTTER, MELTED

VEGETABLE OIL FOR THE PAN

FOR THE FILLING

1¼ CUPS COTTAGE CHEESE

1¼ CUPS RICOTTA CHEESE

1 EGG YOLK, BEATEN

½ CUP SUGAR

¼ TEASPOON GROUND NUTMEG

¼ TEASPOON GROUND CINNAMON

¼ TEASPOON SALT

¼ CUP RAISINS

BUTTER OR VEGETABLE OIL

2 CUPS FRESH BERRIES, RINSED AND SLICED IF NECESSARY

SOUR CREAM FOR GARNISH (OPTIONAL)

TO MAKE THE CREPES

In a medium-size bowl, mix together the flour and salt. Gradually whisk in the eggs and then the milk until smooth. Stir in the melted butter.

Lightly oil a heavy, 8-inch crepe pan, and heat it over medium heat. Pour in about 3 tablespoons of batter, and tilt the pan to spread it evenly over the bottom. Cook the crepe until it's brown on the bottom and no longer runny on the top (don't flip it). Remove it to a plate with a spatula. Cook the rest of the batter, oiling the pan again each time and stacking the finished crepes on top of each other, cooked side up. You'll have about twelve.

(continued)

To Make the Filling

In a medium-size bowl, stir together the cottage cheese, ricotta cheese, egg yolk, sugar, nutmeg, cinnamon, salt, and raisins until well blended.

To Finish the Blintzes

Place a crepe, browned side up, on a flat surface. Place 2 generous tablespoons of filling in a fat line down the center. Fold one side over the filling. Fold both ends in toward the center, and then roll the blintz the long way to seal. Allow 2 or 3 blintzes per person; freeze extras.

Heat a small amount of butter or vegetable oil in a large, heavy skillet over medium heat. Working in batches, place the blintzes in the pan, seam side up, and cook until lightly browned, 3 to 4 minutes. Turn and brown on the other side, 3 to 4 minutes longer. If they have been frozen, brown the blintzes over low heat, covered, and turn them more often.

Transfer the blintzes to a plate, top them with the berries, garnish with sour cream if you like, and serve immediately.

. . . .

Do Ahead: Make the crepes, fill the blintzes, and refrigerate, covered.

In the Morning (about 15 minutes): Brown the blintzes and top with berries. Garnish with sour cream if you really want to indulge.

. . . .

WINTER FRUIT COMPOTE WITH NO-BAKE ORANGE-ALMOND OAT CAKES

In the middle of winter when good fresh fruit is scarce, this dish is a perfect way to start the day. Use prunes, raisins, dried pears, apples, cranberries, cherries, papaya, apricots, peaches, or a combination in the compote. The moist, tasty Orange-Almond Oat Cakes were created by our pastry chef at Flea St., Christine Gutierrez.

5 to 8 servings

For the Fruit Compote

1½ cups dried fruit (see above)

1 cup apple juice

1 cinnamon stick

3 whole cloves

1 to 2 teaspoons balsamic vinegar

Brown sugar (optional)

For the Oat Cakes

½ cup raisins

1 cup apple juice

½ cup applesauce

2 teaspoons molasses

2 tablespoons brown sugar

1 teaspoon grated orange zest

2 cups old-fashioned rolled oats

½ cup chopped raw almonds

To Make the Compote

Combine the dried fruit, apple juice, cinnamon stick, and cloves in a medium-size saucepan. Bring to a simmer over medium-low heat and cook, covered, for about 15 minutes, until the fruit plumps up. Stir in the balsamic vinegar and, if you like, brown sugar to taste.

To Make the Oat Cakes

Pour boiling water to cover over the raisins and let them plump for 10 minutes. Drain.

In a medium-size bowl, stir together the apple juice, applesauce, molasses, brown sugar, and orange zest. Add the oatmeal, almonds, and raisins and blend well.

Divide the mixture into five to eight parts. Roll each in your hand to form a ball. Flatten each ball to form a flat, thick cookie. Let the cakes dry on a rack for an hour or two. Refrigerate them in an airtight container; they will keep for at least a week.

Serve the compote, warm or at room temperature, in small bowls, with an oat cake on the side.

. . . .

Do Ahead: Make the compote and oat cakes, and refrigerate.

In the Morning (5 minutes): Warm the compote on the stove or in the microwave. Take the chill off the oat cakes in a toaster oven or in the microwave, and serve.

. . . .

FRUIT PIZZAS

Fresh warm bread with fruit and cheese—very European. Call it pizza and it couldn't be more American. Using part whole wheat flour creates a slightly heavier, nuttier-tasting crust. I use toasted walnut oil instead of olive oil because I like the way it complements the fruit and cheese. Choose the topping according to the season, using your favorite combination of fruit. Fresh peaches, figs, nectarines, apricots, cherries, and berries of any kind are especially good in summer. In winter, try prunes, raisins, or dried apricots, pears, peaches, figs, and apples.

4 or more servings

FOR THE DOUGH

1 CUP WARM WATER (105 DEGREES)

2 TEASPOONS (1 PACKAGE) ACTIVE DRY YEAST

1 TEASPOON SUGAR

2 TABLESPOONS TOASTED WALNUT OIL

2 CUPS UNBLEACHED WHITE FLOUR

½ CUP WHOLE WHEAT FLOUR

½ TEASPOON SALT

VEGETABLE OIL FOR THE BOWL

CORNMEAL FOR THE PAN

SUMMER FRUIT PIZZA TOPPING OR WINTER

   FRUIT PIZZA TOPPING (RECIPES FOLLOW)

TO MAKE THE DOUGH

Combine the warm water, yeast, and sugar and set aside until the mixture gets foamy. Stir in the walnut oil.

Stir together the flours and salt in the bowl of an electric mixer or food processor. With the machine running, gradually add the yeast mixture. Mix until the ingredients stick together and form a soft ball.

Generously oil a large bowl that has a tight-fitting lid. Put the dough in the bowl, turn it to oil all over, and seal the lid. Refrigerate it for at least 6 hours.

TO ASSEMBLE THE PIZZA

Preheat the oven to 500 degrees. Remove the dough from the refrigerator, and toss it on a well-floured surface, turning to coat both sides. Cut the dough in two, and roll each half into a 10-inch round, flouring the work surface as needed. Sprinkle about a tablespoon of cornmeal on a heavy baking sheet or two pizza pans, and put the dough on them.

Spread the prepared fruit mixture over the dough, leaving a 1-inch border. Sprinkle on the Cheddar cheese or dot on the goat cheese, and sprinkle with a little pepper.

Bake the pizzas for 10 to 15 minutes, until the crust is crisp and lightly browned. Let the pizzas stand for a few minutes before cutting and serving.

Leftovers are great served cold or warmed.

. . . .

DO AHEAD: Make the pizza dough; grate the Cheddar cheese if using; refrigerate. The winter fruit topping can be made the night before and refrigerated. Your choice of fruit will determine if you can make the summer fruit topping ahead; most berries will hold up well in the refrigerator overnight, but any fresh fruit that requires slicing is best fixed just before baking the pizza.

IN THE MORNING (30 TO 45 MINUTES): Preheat the oven. Prepare the fruit topping if necessary. Roll out and top the dough, and bake the pizzas.

. . . .

SUMMER FRUIT PIZZA TOPPING

4 CUPS FRESH FRUIT THAT IS RIPE, FIRM, YET
    SUCCULENT AND JUICY
2 TABLESPOONS FINELY CHOPPED FRESH BASIL
    OR MINT
1 TABLESPOON BALSAMIC VINEGAR
8 OUNCES SHARP CHEDDAR CHEESE, GRATED
FRESHLY GROUND BLACK PEPPER

Clean the fruit, and, if necessary, peel it and cut it into bite-size pieces. Leave berries whole. Toss the fruit with the basil and balsamic vinegar.

WINTER FRUIT PIZZA TOPPING

1 CUP APPLE JUICE
3 CUPS DRIED FRUIT
1 HEAPING TABLESPOON FINELY GRATED
    ORANGE ZEST
½ TEASPOON GROUND CINNAMON
¼ TEASPOON GROUND NUTMEG
PINCH OF GROUND CLOVES
8 OUNCES GOAT CHEESE
FRESHLY GROUND BLACK PEPPER

Bring the apple juice to a boil in a medium-size saucepan. Remove the pan from the heat, stir in the fruit, cover the pan, and set it aside to cool. Stir in the orange zest, cinnamon, nutmeg, and cloves.

WINTHROP MAINE APPLE DUMPLINGS

In the late sixties, at the height of the Vietnam War, I was a draft counselor married to a conscientious objector, who was assigned to a job in Winthrop, Maine. My son was two years old and we lived in a big house on a big lake. I spent much of my time cooking and baking for family and friends, and this dumpling recipe was a favorite. Served warm for breakfast with heavy cream or as a late night snack with a scoop of vanilla ice cream, it was and still is comfort food at its best.

The recipe is simpler than it may look. Basically, you make pie dough, make a stuffing for the apples, peel and core the apples, and cook a syrup to pour over them.

2 breakfast servings, with plenty of leftovers

FOR THE DOUGH

2½ CUPS UNBLEACHED WHITE FLOUR

¼ TEASPOON SALT

1 CUP (2 STICKS) COLD UNSALTED BUTTER

ABOUT ¾ CUP SOUR CREAM

FOR THE APPLES

¼ CUP (½ STICK) UNSALTED BUTTER, SOFTENED

½ CUP LIGHT BROWN SUGAR

1 TEASPOON GROUND CINNAMON

⅛ TEASPOON GROUND NUTMEG

4 TABLESPOONS RAISINS OR CURRANTS

2 TABLESPOONS CHOPPED WALNUTS

8 SMALL BAKING APPLES

FOR THE SYRUP

2 CUPS BROWN SUGAR

1¼ CUPS APPLE JUICE OR WATER

1 TEASPOON VANILLA EXTRACT

TO MAKE THE DOUGH

In a large bowl, blend the flour and salt. In a food processor, pulse the butter into pea-size pieces. Add the flour, and pulse just until blended. Don't overmix; the dough should be very grainy. (Or cut the butter into small pieces and cut it into the flour mixture by hand with a pastry blender.)

Scrape the sour cream into the work bowl, and pulse just until blended. Don't overmix or the dough will be tough. (Or blend in the sour cream by hand.)

Turn the dough onto a well-floured surface, and mold it into a large ball. Flatten the ball and divide it into eight wedges. Form each wedge into a ball, flatten, and refrigerate.

To Prepare the Apples

Stir together the butter, brown sugar, cinnamon, nutmeg, raisins, and walnuts. Set aside.

Peel and core the apples, leaving them whole. Set them in a deep baking dish, and spoon the filling into the cavities.

Preheat the oven to 350 degrees.

Roll out the dough balls into circles 6 or 7 inches across, and wrap them completely around the stuffed apples. Return the apples to the baking dish, and put them in the oven. Let them bake for about 10 minutes while you prepare the syrup.

To Make the Syrup

Stir together the brown sugar, apple juice, and vanilla in a saucepan. Bring the mixture to a simmer over medium heat and cook until slightly thickened, about 8 minutes.

Remove the apples from the oven and pour on the syrup. Bake them for 30 to 45 minutes more, until tender, basting every 10 minutes with the syrup.

Serve hot, covered with syrup.

. . . .

DO AHEAD: Make and bake the dumplings, and refrigerate, covered with foil.

IN THE MORNING (30 TO 40 MINUTES): Preheat the oven to 375 degrees, and reheat the dumplings, covered, for about 30 minutes.

. . . .

ASPARAGUS, SUN-DRIED TOMATO, WILD RICE, AND SPRING GARLIC FRITTATA (PAGE 49)

Eggs

It wasn't that long ago that people not only had backyards, but chickens in them, too. Eggs had to be collected daily. It seems natural, a matter of course, that newly laid eggs, often still warm, would have found their way into the morning meal.

Fresh eggs were one of the things I had in mind when I bought a bungalow in Palo Alto, California, a couple of years ago. The area around the house, now part of the town proper, used to be farmland, though no one thinks of it that way anymore. There is a field behind the house, where I wanted to build raised flower beds and keep a few chickens. To my surprise—and the surprise of my neighbors—I am permitted six chickens. None can be roosters, out of consideration for those, unlike my family, who would rather not start their day with crowing. But I wanted fresh eggs and now I have them.

Like any other ingredient, fresh, farm-raised eggs make all the difference in the world. If you have access to them, by all means use them. If you don't, you'll still be delighted with these recipes. Using seasonal produce, from your garden or a local farmer's market, will bring out the best in each dish. In Scrambled Eggs on Caramelized Onions, for example, or Fresh Herb, Watercress, and Spring Garlic Omelet, the difference between outrageously good and simply good lies in the true, full-bodied flavors of the ingredients.

Family Favorites

MY DAD'S FISH AND EGGS

Every summer when I was growing up, our family went on vacation to Atlantic City. My dad would head down to the local fish market each day at the crack of dawn to buy just-caught fish fillets. Then, starting about 6 A.M., he would fry up his fish and eggs in the small kitchen of our motel room. When I was a child I hated waking to the smell of his invention. Today, I love it.

4 servings

1 POUND FRESH FLAKY WHITE FISH FILLETS SUCH AS FLOUNDER, COD, OR RED SNAPPER

½ CUP UNBLEACHED WHITE FLOUR

1 TEASPOON SALT

½ TEASPOON FRESHLY GROUND PEPPER

PINCH OF CAYENNE

10 EGGS

2 TABLESPOONS WATER

2 CUPS TOASTED BREAD CRUMBS

2 TO 4 TABLESPOONS VEGETABLE OIL, SUCH AS CANOLA

2 TO 3 TABLESPOONS UNSALTED BUTTER

1 MEDIUM YELLOW ONION, CHOPPED

½ CUP GRATED PARMESAN CHEESE PLUS MORE FOR GARNISH

CAYENNE FOR GARNISH (OPTIONAL)

⅓ CUP MANGO CHUTNEY (STORE-BOUGHT OR HOMEMADE)

CHOPPED PARSLEY FOR GARNISH

Rinse the fish, and remove any bones. In a shallow dish like a pie plate, stir together the flour, salt, pepper, and cayenne. In another shallow dish, whisk 2 eggs with about 2 tablespoons water. Put the bread crumbs in a third dish, and set out two empty plates.

Dust each piece of fish generously with the flour mixture, dip it in the egg wash, and roll it in the bread crumbs to coat thoroughly. Set aside on a plate until ready to fry.

Heat 2 tablespoons of the oil in a large, heavy skillet over medium-high heat until it's almost smoking. Working in batches, and adding more oil to the pan as needed, fry the fish until lightly browned on both sides and cooked through, about 4 to 5 minutes per side. Transfer it to one of the clean plates, and break into bite-size pieces.

Whisk the remaining 8 eggs together, and wipe out the skillet with paper towels.

Melt the butter in the skillet over medium heat, and sauté the onion until slightly softened, about 5 minutes. Add the whisked eggs, and then the fish. As the eggs cook, lift the edges so that the uncooked portion flows to the outside; don't scramble them. When the eggs are almost set, sprinkle on the Parmesan. Continue cooking until eggs are set and the cheese is melted. Cut into four wedges, turn, and brown lightly on the other side.

Divide among four plates. Sprinkle each portion with more Parmesan and a little cayenne if you choose. Spoon a generous dollop of chutney in the center, sprinkle with chopped parsley, and serve immediately.

....

DO AHEAD: Fry and break up the fish, chop the onions, and refrigerate, securely covered.

IN THE MORNING (ABOUT 10 MINUTES): Sauté the onions, and cook and garnish the eggs as directed.

....

MY MOM'S NURTURING MASHED SOFT-COOKED EGGS

My mom was a wonderful nurturer and home nurse. I was home sick a lot with tonsillitis, and she would bring my meals on a bed tray—gentle food like this dish that seemed to work as well as the penicillin. These eggs are like many childhood memories, personal, warming, and full of love. They may not have the eye appeal of haute cuisine, but they sure taste good especially when you're sick. It is important that some of the yolk be soft so you can mash it with the buttered bread.

2 servings

4 TO 6 EGGS, AT ROOM TEMPERATURE
4 SLICES OF WHITE BREAD
3 TABLESPOONS BUTTER, SOFTENED
LOTS OF SALT AND FRESHLY GROUND PEPPER

Put the eggs in a saucepan. Add water to cover and bring it to a gentle boil over medium heat. Immediately reduce the heat to a simmer.

From the time the water first boils, simmer 2 to 4 minutes for soft-cooked eggs (very loose whites, soft yolks) and 4 to 6 minutes for medium soft-cooked eggs (harder whites, soft yolks). Smaller and/or room-temperature eggs will take less time; larger and/or cold ones more time.

While the eggs are cooking, remove the crusts from the bread and spread the slices with butter. Tear them into pieces and put them in two bowls.

Drain the eggs, and holding them with a towel, crack them in half over the bread, and scoop out the yolks and whites with a spoon. Stir gently with a fork, mashing the bread with the eggs. Season with salt and pepper, and serve immediately.

....

IN THE MORNING: This dish is so simple you can prepare it in 10 minutes.

....

JOSH'S CHILAQUILES
WITH AVOCADO

Popular in Mexico, this version of eggs scrambled with tortilla strips is a favorite of my older boy, Joshua. He lives in Japan now, and whenever he comes home for a visit I try to have the ingredients ready and waiting in my refrigerator. I always make extra. Leftovers are great eaten at room temperature—perfect food for a lazy, stay-at-home Saturday.

4 servings, with leftovers

3 MEDIUM FLOUR OR CORN TORTILLAS

3 TABLESPOONS VEGETABLE OIL

1 MEDIUM ONION, CHOPPED

10 EGGS, BEATEN

1 MEDIUM TOMATO, SEEDED AND COARSELY CHOPPED

4 TO 6 OUNCES JACK, PEPPER JACK, OR SOFT MEXICAN CHEESE, CUT INTO ½-INCH CHUNKS

½ CUP CHOPPED CILANTRO PLUS MORE FOR GARNISH (OPTIONAL)

1 AVOCADO, PEELED AND DICED

SALT AND PEPPER

SALSA, SOUR CREAM, AND CAYENNE FOR GARNISH (OPTIONAL)

Slice the tortillas in half, and then into ½-inch-wide strips. Set aside.

Heat a large sauté pan over medium heat, and add the oil. When it's hot, sauté the onion until wilted, about 3 minutes. Add the tortilla strips and brown lightly, turning frequently.

Whisk the eggs with the tomato, and pour them into the pan. Using a spatula, push the cooked eggs toward the center, turning by large tablespoonfuls. Try not to scramble the eggs or break up the tortilla strips.

When the eggs are nearly cooked but still a bit runny, stir in the cheese, cilantro, avocado, and salt and pepper to taste. Turn the heat to low, cover the pan, and cook for a minute longer. Take the pan off the heat and let it sit for a few minutes, until the cheese is melted.

Garnish with salsa, sour cream, cayenne, and extra cilantro, if you like.

....

DO AHEAD: Chop onion, tomato, and cilantro. Cut up the tortillas and cheese. Peel and cut up avocado; to keep it from browning, store it with the avocado pit and squeeze a bit of lime or lemon juice over the top. Refrigerate all of these ingredients in individual bowls, covered.

IN THE MORNING (ABOUT 10 MINUTES): Whisk and cook the eggs as directed.

....

JONAH'S EGG-IN-THE-EYE OVER RATATOUILLE

My younger son's favorite fast-and-easy breakfast is egg-in-the-eye (aka toad-in-the-hole; anybody know any other names for this old favorite?). I always find myself hoping for leftovers, but Jonah has been known to take off on his bike with the last bites in one hand.

Egg-in-the-eye is not a glorious dish. It might be garnished with a touch of catsup, but usually the only variation is how hard or soft to cook the yolks on that particular morning.

When making it for a grown-up, I like to take it a step further. The inspiration for pairing it with ratatouille came, of course, from pulling leftovers out of the refrigerator one morning. Oozing yolks and crisp, buttery, panfried bread seem to melt into the juicy ratatouille. Spike it with a bit of cayenne if you want to add a little zest to your morning in bed.

2 servings

2 TO 4 SLICES WHOLE WHEAT OR WHITE BREAD

2 TABLESPOONS UNSALTED BUTTER

2 TO 4 EGGS

2 CUPS RATATOUILLE, WARMED (RECIPE FOLLOWS)

GRATED PARMESAN CHEESE FOR GARNISH (OPTIONAL)

Cut a large circle or square out of the middle of each slice of bread.

Melt the butter in a large, heavy skillet over medium heat. Put the bread slices and holes in the pan. When they're lightly coated with butter, flip them over.

Crack an egg into the hole of each slice. Cover the pan and cook for about 3 minutes. Flip the bread and eggs. Remove the holes when browned.

Spoon the ratatouille onto two plates. When the eggs are cooked to your liking, place one or two eggs-in-the-eye on each plate. Top the eggs with the browned bread holes, and sprinkle with grated Parmesan cheese if you choose. Serve immediately.

. . . .

DO AHEAD: Make the ratatouille. Refrigerate, covered, overnight; the flavor improves. Cut the holes in the bread and store in a plastic bag.

IN THE MORNING: Warm the ratatouille. Cook the bread and eggs as directed.

. . . .

RATATOUILLE

This makes 6 or 8 cups, enough for several break-fasts. Or serve the extra with pasta or polenta and a salad for lunch.

2 MEDIUM TOMATOES, PEELED AND SEEDED IF
 YOU CHOOSE
1 SMALL EGGPLANT
1 MEDIUM SWEET RED PEPPER, SEEDED
1 MEDIUM ONION
2 MEDIUM ZUCCHINI OR YELLOW SUMMER SQUASH
2 TABLESPOONS EXTRA-VIRGIN OLIVE OIL
4 GARLIC CLOVES, FINELY CHOPPED
LEAVES FROM 5 OR 6 SPRIGS FRESH OREGANO,
 OR ¾ TEASPOON DRIED OREGANO
⅓ CUP DRY RED WINE
¾ CUP COARSELY CHOPPED FRESH BASIL
SALT AND FRESHLY GROUND PEPPER
CAYENNE (OPTIONAL)

Chop the tomatoes, eggplant, red pepper, onion, and zucchini into 1-inch cubes.

In a large saucepan, heat the olive oil with the garlic over medium heat. Add all the vegetables. Bring to a simmer and cook, uncovered, over low heat, stirring occasionally, for 30 to 45 minutes, until the vegetables are very soft. Stir in the oregano, wine, basil, salt, pepper, and, if using, cayenne to taste. Let it sit off the heat for at least 10 minutes before serving.

SCOTCH EGGS WITH CURRIED CHUTNEY–YOGURT SAUCE

This dish got a unanimous thumbs-up from my restaurant staff. It would make a wonderful buffet item because it's delicious hot or at room temperature.

2 hearty or 4 light servings

FOR THE CURRIED CHUTNEY–YOGURT SAUCE

½ CUP PLAIN YOGURT
¼ CUP SOUR CREAM
1 TABLESPOON CURRY POWDER
1 TEASPOON CUMIN
2 GENEROUS TABLESPOONS MANGO CHUTNEY
1 TEASPOON MINCED CHIVES

FOR THE EGGS

2 EGGS, BEATEN
2 CUPS TOASTED BREAD CRUMBS
1 POUND BULK PORK, TURKEY, OR CHICKEN
 SAUSAGE
2 TABLESPOONS GRATED ONION
2 TABLESPOONS GRATED CARROT
1 TEASPOON RUBBED SAGE
1 GENEROUS TABLESPOON UNBLEACHED
 WHITE FLOUR
4 HARD-COOKED EGGS, PEELED (SEE NOTE)

To Make the Sauce

Stir together the yogurt, sour cream, curry powder, cumin, chutney, and chives. Refrigerate.

To Make the Eggs

Preheat the oven to 375 degrees. Cover a small baking sheet with parchment paper or a light coating of oil. Put the beaten eggs in one shallow dish and the bread crumbs in another.

Mix the sausage well with the onion, carrot, sage, and flour. Using your hands, mold a quarter of the sausage mixture around each of the hard-cooked eggs, encasing the egg completely.

Roll the sausage balls in the beaten egg and then in the crumbs, coating them well. Bake them on the prepared sheet for about 15 minutes, until the sausage is browned and cooked through.

Serve hot or at room temperature with a generous dollop of Curried Chutney–Yogurt Sauce.

NOTE: To cook the eggs, put them in a saucepan with water to cover. Bring it just to a boil, remove the pan from the heat, and let it sit, covered, for 15 minutes. Drain the eggs and run cold water over them until they're cool enough to peel.

....

DO AHEAD: Make the yogurt sauce. Cook the eggs. Make the sausage mixture. Cover, dip, and coat the eggs. Refrigerate, covered, overnight.

IN THE MORNING (20 TO 35 MINUTES): Preheat the oven and bake the Scotch eggs. Because they have been refrigerated, they may take as long as 30 minutes.

....

BREAKFAST BURRITOS

This hefty handful of a breakfast will keep man, woman, or child satisfied for hours. If you're not serving it in bed, set out all the ingredients buffet-style, and let others assemble their own burritos. This recipe was created with a slumber party in mind, but can be adapted accordingly for two.

6 servings

6 LARGE FLOUR TORTILLAS

2 TABLESPOONS VEGETABLE OIL

1 MEDIUM ONION, COARSELY CHOPPED

1 POUND POTATOES, SCRUBBED AND COARSELY
   CHOPPED

SALT AND FRESHLY GROUND PEPPER

2 CUPS COOKED PINTO OR BLACK BEANS

1 TEASPOON GROUND CUMIN

1 CUP SALSA

½ CUP CHOPPED CILANTRO

6 LARGE EGGS, BEATEN

8 OUNCES GRATED JACK, CHEDDAR, OR FRESH
   MEXICAN CHEESE (QUESO BLANCO)

OPTIONAL ADDITIONS

GUACAMOLE

SOUR CREAM

CHOPPED GRILLED CHICKEN, PORK, STEAK,
   SEAFOOD, OR CHORIZO

CHOPPED GREEN ONION, TOMATO, CILANTRO,
   AND/OR BLACK OLIVES

PICKLED JALAPEÑOS

SEASONED OR PLAIN COOKED RICE

Preheat the oven to 350 degrees. Wrap the tortillas in aluminum foil.

Heat an ovenproof skillet over medium heat, and add the oil. When it's hot, sauté the onion until soft, about 5 minutes. Stir in the potatoes and sauté until cooked, 10 to 15 minutes. Season the potato mixture with plenty of salt and pepper, and put it in the oven to keep warm.

Stir together the beans, cumin, and a few tablespoons of the salsa in either a microwave-safe or ovenproof dish, depending on how you intend to heat it. Heat it until hot in the microwave, 5 minutes, or on the stovetop, 10 to 15 minutes. Stir in the cilantro and set it aside, covered.

Return the skillet with the potato mixture to the stovetop over medium heat. Pour in the beaten eggs. Stir the eggs, scrambling them, until they are cooked to your liking.

While the eggs are cooking, warm the tortillas in the oven for 5 minutes.

To make a basic burrito, sprinkle a small hand-ful of cheese over the center of the tortilla. Top the cheese with generous portions of the hot potato and bean mixtures. Spoon on some of the remaining salsa and any additions and garnishes you like. Fold over two sides and roll like a jelly roll.

....

DO AHEAD: Chop and cook the potatoes and onions. Stir together the beans, cumin, and salsa. Grate the cheese, and prepare any additions or garnishes.

IN THE MORNING (20 TO 30 MINUTES): Preheat the oven and warm the tortillas. Heat the seasoned beans and stir in the cilantro. Heat any meat you're using. Heat the potato mixture in the skillet, and cook the eggs as directed. Assemble the burritos or set out the ingredients buffet-style.

....

SCRAMBLED EGGS ON CARAMELIZED ONIONS

See frontispiece

This is one of my favorite breakfasts. I always have butter in the freezer, an egg or two in the refrigerator, and an onion in the vegetable bin. A thick slice of toast with homemade jam makes it complete.

2 servings

3 TABLESPOONS UNSALTED BUTTER

2 MEDIUM ONIONS, SLICED VERY THIN

SALT

4 TO 6 EGGS, BEATEN

FRESHLY GROUND PEPPER

2 TABLESPOONS CHOPPED CHIVES OR CHIVE BLOSSOMS

Melt 1 tablespoon of the butter in a heavy skil-let over medium heat. Reduce the heat to low and add the onions. Cover the pan and cook until the onions are very soft and caramel-colored, about 5 minutes. Season to taste with salt, and set aside, covered.

Melt the remaining 2 tablespoons butter in a small skillet over medium heat. Pour in the beaten eggs, and add salt and pepper to taste. Scramble to desired doneness.

Divide the onions between two dinner plates, spreading them to create a bed. Spoon the eggs on top, and garnish with the chives. Serve immediately.

....

DO AHEAD: Sauté the onions. Chop the chives. Cover and refrigerate separately overnight.

IN THE MORNING (ABOUT 10 MINUTES): Warm the onions, and cook the eggs as directed.

....

SWEET PEPPER, SHIITAKE MUSHROOM, AND LEEK BREAKFAST SANDWICH

I had my first breakfast sandwich when I was thirteen and my parents took me and my two brothers to Europe with a group of antique car collectors. My dad owned a 1926 Cadillac and a 1929 Reo Flying Cloud sports coupe. A friend of his, Mrs. Dent, made breakfast sandwiches for all of us to eat on the way to the airport. I don't remember exactly what was in them, but they were drenched with homemade olive oil. Though the flavor was foreign to me as breakfast food, I loved it. This sandwich reminds me of hers, and of that memorable vacation.

2 servings

2 TABLESPOONS EXTRA-VIRGIN OLIVE OIL
1 CUP THINLY SLICED SHIITAKE MUSHROOMS
½ MEDIUM SWEET RED PEPPER
½ CUP SLICED LEEKS (WHITE PART ONLY)
2 GARLIC CLOVES, MINCED
1 TEASPOON CHOPPED FRESH ROSEMARY, OR
  ½ TEASPOON DRIED ROSEMARY
2 TABLESPOONS DRY RED WINE (OPTIONAL)
4 EGGS, BEATEN
SALT AND FRESHLY GROUND PEPPER
3 OUNCES SWISS, MOZZARELLA, JACK, OR
  OTHER MELTING CHEESE, CUBED
2 CRUSTY HARD ROLLS
CHOPPED PARSLEY FOR GARNISH

Heat a skillet over medium heat, and add 1 tablespoon of the oil. When it's hot, sauté the mushrooms, pepper, leeks, and garlic until soft, about 5 minutes. Stir in the rosemary and wine, and cook a little longer, until the wine evaporates.

Pour the eggs into the pan, and season with salt and pepper to taste. Scramble, adding the cheese when the eggs are about three-quarters done. Cook, stirring, until the eggs are done to your liking.

Remove the pan from the heat, and let it stand, covered, until the cheese melts, 3 or 4 minutes. Cut a slit in each roll and stuff it with the egg filling. Garnish with parsley, and let it sit for 5 minutes before serving so the rolls absorb the flavor.

. . . .

DO AHEAD: Cook the vegetables, cube the cheese, and refrigerate, covered, overnight.

IN THE MORNING (ABOUT 15 MINUTES): Reheat the vegetables. Cook the eggs and assemble the sandwich as directed.

. . . .

Fried Pasta and Eggs with Green Onions, Garlic, and Asiago Cheese

The pasta really stretches the eggs in this savory pancake. It's great for brunch or for a bunch of hungry teenagers after a slumber party. In summer, garnish it generously with chopped fresh tomatoes, basil, and red onion. In cold weather, try sun-dried tomatoes, roasted garlic, and rosemary or oregano.

2 servings

4 EGGS

3 TABLESPOONS GRATED ASIAGO OR PARMESAN CHEESE

⅓ CUP CHOPPED GREEN ONIONS

¾ TEASPOON SALT

GENEROUS GRINDING OF PEPPER

2 TABLESPOONS LIGHT OLIVE OIL

2 GARLIC CLOVES, MINCED

1½ CUPS COOKED THIN EGG NOODLES, RICE NOODLES, OR BUCKWHEAT NOODLES

CHOPPED TOMATOES AND HERBS FOR GARNISH (SEE ABOVE)

Whisk the eggs with the cheese, onions, salt, and pepper. Set aside.

Heat a medium-size skillet over medium heat and add the oil. When it's hot, stir in the garlic and pasta, and sauté until lightly browned, 3 to 4 minutes. Flip to the other side and sauté a few minutes more.

Pour the egg mixture over the pasta. Stir a bit, moving the eggs around to cook them in the center. When the eggs are still slightly runny, stop stirring and let them set and brown slightly. Flip over and brown on the other side.

Transfer to a large plate, and top with tomatoes and herbs.

....

DO AHEAD: Combine the cheese, onions, and seasoning. Cook the pasta, and mix it with the minced garlic. Chop the tomatoes and herbs. Cover and refrigerate each mixture separately.

IN THE MORNING (ABOUT 15 MINUTES): Cook the pasta with the eggs as directed.

....

STEAMED EGGS WITH QUICK RANCHERO SAUCE

Serve this simple, lively dish with grilled chorizo or spicy poultry sausage and steaming hot tortillas. In the summer, a fresh ear of corn complements it beautifully.

2 servings

3 OR 4 SERRANO OR OTHER MEDIUM-HOT FRESH CHILES

2½ POUNDS RIPE RED OR GOLDEN TOMATOES

VEGETABLE OIL

½ CUP COARSELY CHOPPED ONION

3 GARLIC CLOVES, COARSELY CHOPPED

1½ TEASPOONS CUMIN

¼ CUP CHOPPED CILANTRO

SALT AND FRESHLY GROUND PEPPER

4 EGGS

2 TO 4 LARGE FLOUR OR CORN TORTILLAS

Preheat the broiler or the oven to 450 degrees.

Spread the peppers in a baking dish and broil or bake them, turning often, until the skins blister and blacken. Transfer them to an airtight container. When cool enough to handle, peel, stem, and seed the peppers.

While the peppers are cooling, wash the tomatoes and remove the stem ends. Lightly oil a baking dish, and spread the tomatoes, onion, and garlic in it. Broil or bake at 450 degrees, turning occasionally, until the skins of the tomatoes blister, about 20 minutes. When cool enough to handle, peel the tomatoes, cut them in half, and scoop out the seeds.

Transfer the tomatoes, onion, garlic, and all the pan juices to a food processor or blender. Add the seeded peppers and the cumin and cilantro. Puree. Season to taste with salt and pepper.

Reduce the oven temperature to 375 degrees. Spoon about 1 cup of sauce into a small, heavy baking dish. Crack the eggs into the sauce, allowing enough room so that they don't run together. Spoon a little more sauce on top of each egg, and bake until they're done the way you like. Medium-soft eggs will take about 10 minutes.

While the eggs are baking, wrap the tortillas in aluminum foil and put them in the oven for about 5 minutes to warm.

Transfer the cooked eggs and sauce to plates, and serve with the warm tortillas.

....

DO AHEAD: Make and refrigerate the ranchero sauce.

IN THE MORNING (20 TO 25 MINUTES): Reheat the sauce, and bake the eggs as directed. Warm the tortillas.

....

For Special Occasions

CRAB CAKES IN CHIVE CUSTARD

Sensual memories are made of this: elegant crab cakes in velvety custard served to your lover in bed.

2 servings

8 OUNCES FRESH DUNGENESS OR OTHER TOP-QUALITY CRABMEAT

2 TO 3 TABLESPOONS CHOPPED SWEET RED PEPPER

1 GREEN ONION, MINCED

3 TABLESPOONS MAYONNAISE

½ TEASPOON MINCED LEMON ZEST

GENEROUS PINCH OF CAYENNE

SALT

1 CUP FRESH BREAD CRUMBS

¼ CUP VEGETABLE OIL

3 LARGE EGGS

1 EGG YOLK

2 CUPS WHOLE MILK

2 TABLESPOONS CHOPPED CHIVES

½ TEASPOON SWEET PAPRIKA

In a medium-size bowl, thoroughly combine the crab, red pepper, green onion, mayonnaise, lemon zest, cayenne, and salt to taste. Add more mayonnaise if needed to make it stick together. Form the mixture into four patties about 2 inches in diameter and ¾ inch thick. Dip them in the bread crumbs, coating thoroughly.

Heat a large, heavy skillet over medium-high heat, and add the oil. When it's hot, sauté the crab cakes until lightly browned, 3 to 4 minutes per side. Transfer to two shallow, 3- or 4-cup baking dishes (put two crab cakes in each).

Preheat the oven to 325 degrees.

Whisk together the eggs, egg yolk, milk, chives, paprika, and ¼ to ½ teaspoon salt. Pour half this custard mixture into each baking dish.

Place the dishes in a large pan, and set it in the oven. Pour hot water into the pan so that it reaches halfway up the sides of the baking dishes. Bake for about 45 minutes, until the custard is firm.

To serve, set each hot custard dish on a heatproof plate lined with a folded cloth napkin. Use the napkin to support and maneuver the custard dish without burning your hands.

. . . .

DO AHEAD: Form the crab cakes and coat them with bread crumbs. Whisk together the custard ingredients. Cover and refrigerate all.

IN THE MORNING (ABOUT 1 HOUR): Sauté the crab cakes and bake the custard as directed.

. . . .

POTATO-ONION NESTS WITH CREAMED SPINACH AND EGGS

This dish is for a cold, rainy morning when you want to indulge, when you want to fill someone's belly with something rich, something warming, something that took a little extra time to prepare. It's for one of those delectable mornings when the chores don't get done but the glow of the good life is evident on your face the whole day through. You can substitute a 16-ounce package of frozen spinach, thawed and squeezed dry, for the fresh.

2 servings

FOR THE POTATO-ONION NESTS

VEGETABLE OIL

1 CUP GRATED BAKED POTATO

2 TABLESPOONS GRATED RED ONION

½ TEASPOON SALT

FOR THE CREAMED SPINACH

2 TABLESPOONS BUTTER

3 TABLESPOONS UNBLEACHED WHITE FLOUR

1 TO 1½ CUPS MILK (WHOLE OR 2 PERCENT)

¼ CUP GRATED ASIAGO OR CHEDDAR CHEESE

⅛ TEASPOON DRY MUSTARD

GENEROUS PINCH OF FRESHLY GROUND NUTMEG

SALT AND FRESHLY GROUND PEPPER

1 POUND FRESH SPINACH, STEAMED, CHOPPED, AND SQUEEZED DRY

TO FINISH THE DISH

4 EGGS

TO MAKE THE POTATO-ONION NESTS

Preheat the oven or toaster oven to 450 degrees. Oil two 1-cup ramekins or custard cups.

Mix the potato, onion, and salt together, and divide it between the ramekins. Press it into the sides and bottoms, forming cups about ½ inch thick. Brush lightly with oil. Bake for 30 to 40 minutes, until lightly browned and crisp. Set aside on a cooling rack.

TO MAKE THE CREAMED SPINACH

While the potato cups are baking, melt the butter in a heavy saucepan over medium heat. Stir in the flour; when it begins to bubble, reduce the heat to low and cook, whisking constantly, for about 3 minutes. Gradually pour in the milk, still whisking, and simmer until thickened, about 5 minutes. Add the cheese, and stir until melted. Stir in the mustard, nutmeg, salt and pepper to taste, and the spinach. Remove the pan from the heat.

Preheat the broiler.

TO FINISH THE DISH

Poach or lightly scramble the eggs in a little butter, leaving them slightly underdone. Divide the eggs between the potato nests, and cover with warm creamed spinach. Put the ramekins under the broiler for a minute or two, until lightly browned. Serve immediately.

....

DO AHEAD: Assemble the potato nests, make the creamed spinach, and refrigerate separately, covered.

IN THE MORNING (30 TO 40 MINUTES): Bake the nests, reheat the creamed spinach, cook the eggs, and finish the dish as directed.

....

Omelets, Tortas, and Frittatas

If you've mastered the art of flipping omelets to cook both sides before adding the filling, go for it! If not, omelets, like tortas and frittatas, work out just as well finished in a 400-degree oven. Cook until done throughout. Cooking time varies, depending on the thickness of the eggs. Omelets can be done in 3 to 4 minutes. Tortas and frittatas can take up to 20 minutes.

SMOKED SALMON, AVOCADO, CHEDDAR, AND GREEN ONION OMELET

Thinking of this luscious omelet makes my mouth water. It pairs perfectly with toasted bagels and cream cheese and a rosé champagne or a blush California sparkling wine.

2 servings

6 EGGS

2 OR 3 GREEN ONIONS, THINLY SLICED

2 TABLESPOONS CHOPPED FRESH CHERVIL OR PARSLEY

2 TABLESPOONS UNSALTED BUTTER OR VEGETABLE OIL

3 OUNCES CHEDDAR CHEESE, GRATED

4 TO 6 OUNCES SMOKED SALMON, TORN INTO BITE-SIZE PIECES

½ LARGE OR 1 SMALL AVOCADO, PEELED AND CUT INTO CHUNKS

SOUR CREAM, CHOPPED RED ONION, AND CAPERS FOR GARNISH (OPTIONAL)

Preheat the oven or the broiler to 400 degrees.

Beat the eggs with the green onions and chervil.

Melt half the butter over medium heat in an ovenproof 8- to 10-inch skillet. Pour in half the egg mixture. Use a spatula to push the cooked egg toward the center, tilting the pan in a circular motion so that the uncooked egg flows to the outside.

When the eggs are no longer runny, sprinkle on half the cheese, and put the pan in the oven or under the broiler for a minute or two until the cheese melts and the omelet is lightly browned.

Transfer the omelet to a plate, cover it to keep warm, and cook the second one in the same way.

Arrange half the salmon and avocado on one side of each omelet. Fold the other side over the filling, and garnish if you like with sour cream, red onion, and capers.

. . . .

DO AHEAD: Chop the green onions and the herbs, grate the cheese. Tear the smoked salmon. Chop the avocado and store with its pit. Cover everything and refrigerate. Store garnishes in small serving bowls to serve next to the omelet in the morning.

IN THE MORNING (ABOUT 20 MINUTES): Cook the omelets as directed.

. . . .

TOMATO, AVOCADO, AND BASIL OMELET OVER GRILLED BREAD

Sweet, juicy tomato, avocado, and basil are folded into an omelet and served on garlicky grilled bread. Picture sitting on a sunporch in your nightgown, still waking up, and having this dish placed before you.

2 servings

3 TABLESPOONS EXTRA-VIRGIN OLIVE OIL

2 GARLIC CLOVES, SLICED

FOUR 1- TO 1½-INCH-THICK SLICES ITALIAN BREAD

6 EGGS

3 TABLESPOONS CHOPPED ITALIAN PARSLEY PLUS MORE FOR GARNISH (OPTIONAL)

SALT AND FRESHLY GROUND PEPPER

4 TO 6 THICK SLICES RIPE TOMATO

1 SMALL AVOCADO, PEELED AND SLICED

6 TO 8 BASIL LEAVES, CHOPPED, PLUS MORE FOR GARNISH (OPTIONAL)

GRATED PROVOLONE CHEESE (OPTIONAL)

Preheat the broiler or oven to 400 degrees.

In a small bowl, combine 1 tablespoon of the olive oil with the garlic, and let it sit for 10 minutes. Brush one side of the bread with the seasoned oil, and put it under the broiler until lightly browned, 2 or 3 minutes. Set the bread aside, and leave the broiler on.

Whisk the eggs with the parsley and salt and pepper to taste.

Heat an 8- to 10-inch skillet over medium heat, and add 1 tablespoon of oil, swirling the pan to coat the bottom. Pour in half the egg mixture. Use a spatula to push the cooked egg toward the center, tilting the pan in a circular motion so that the uncooked egg flows to the outside.

When the eggs are no longer runny, remove the omelet from the heat and arrange half the tomato, avocado, and basil on top. Put under the broiler until the eggs are cooked and the vegetables are warm, about 2 minutes.

Using a spatula, fold the omelet in half, sprinkle it with cheese if you wish, and then fold it in quarters. Cover it to keep warm, and cook the second omelet in the same way.

Arrange the grilled bread on two plates, and put the omelets on top. Garnish with basil or parsley if you choose. Serve immediately.

....

DO AHEAD: Chop the parsley and basil, grate the cheese if using, slice the tomato; refrigerate, covered. Chop the avocado and store with its pit, refrigerated. Combine the olive oil and garlic, and cover.

IN THE MORNING (ABOUT 20 MINUTES): Slice and grill the bread, and cook the omelet as directed.

....

FRESH HERB, WATERCRESS, AND SPRING GARLIC OMELET

Imagine the light of a fresh spring morning beaming through an open window, touching cotton sheets crumpled into softness after a perfect night's sleep. This uncomplicated omelet embodies the sprouting of new green growth, and it makes a romantic welcome for the loveliest season. Garnish it with watercress, cracked black pepper, and sliced apricots or peaches topped with a bit of brown sugar and sour cream.

2 servings

1 TABLESPOON LIGHT OLIVE OIL

4 TENDER SHOOTS OF GREEN GARLIC, BABY LEEKS, OR GREEN ONIONS, THINLY SLICED

6 EGGS

¼ CUP CHOPPED TARRAGON, CHERVIL, OR OTHER SPRING HERBS

2 SMALL HANDFULS OF WATERCRESS LEAVES, CHOPPED

2 TABLESPOONS UNSALTED BUTTER

GARNISHES (OPTIONAL; SEE ABOVE)

If using, preheat the oven or the broiler to 400 degrees.

Heat an 8- or 10-inch skillet over low heat, and add the olive oil. When it's hot, add the garlic and cook just until softened, about 3 minutes.

Scrape the garlic into a bowl. Add the eggs, herbs, and watercress, and whisk well.

Return the skillet to the stove, and melt half the butter over medium heat, swirling the pan to coat the bottom. Pour in half the egg mixture. Use a spatula to push the cooked egg toward the center, tilting the pan in a circular motion so that the uncooked egg flows to the outside.

When the eggs are no longer runny, either flip the omelet or put it in the oven or under the broiler to finish cooking. Transfer the omelet to a plate, cover it to keep warm, and cook the second one in the same way.

Fold the omelets in half, garnish if you choose, and serve immediately.

. . . .

DO AHEAD: Chop the garlic, herbs, and watercress. Prepare any garnishes. Cover and refrigerate.

IN THE MORNING (ABOUT 20 MINUTES): Cook the omelets as directed.

. . . .

Bacon, Cheddar, Chard, Leek, and Chutney Omelet

This combination of ingredients, particularly the bacon and chutney, is always welcome by the men in my life.

2 servings

- **3 strips thick-sliced bacon (preferably nitrate-free)**
- **1 tablespoon butter or vegetable oil (optional)**
- **½ cup thinly sliced leeks (white part only)**
- **1 to 1½ cups packed thinly sliced red or green chard**
- **1 to 2 tablespoons chopped fresh oregano or marjoram leaves**
- **Salt and freshly ground pepper**
- **5 eggs, beaten**
- **2 tablespoons or more grated Cheddar cheese**
- **2 to 3 tablespoons chutney**
- **2 generous tablespoons sour cream**

Cut the bacon into 1-inch pieces, and fry it in a skillet over medium heat until crisp. Remove with a slotted spoon and drain on paper towels. (If you prefer not to cook the vegetables in bacon fat, drain and wipe out the pan, and use the butter or vegetable oil.)

Reduce the heat to low, and sauté the leeks until soft, about 5 minutes. Stir in the chard and oregano. Cover the pan and cook until wilted, about 3 minutes. Season to taste with salt and pepper.

Preheat the broiler.

Add the eggs to the pan. Use a spatula to push the cooked egg toward the center, tilting the pan in a circular motion so that the uncooked egg flows to the outside.

When the eggs are no longer runny, sprinkle on the cheese. Place the pan under the broiler until the cheese is melted and the eggs are barely firm, about 1 minute; do not overcook.

Sprinkle the omelet with bacon, and spread it with chutney. Fold it in half, and slide or flip it onto a large serving plate. Garnish with sour cream and freshly ground pepper, and serve.

....

Do Ahead: Fry the bacon. Cook the leek-chard mixture. Grate the cheese. Refrigerate separately, covered.

In the Morning (about 20 minutes): Rewarm the sautéed vegetables in a skillet, and complete the omelet as directed.

....

WILTED GREENS AND GOAT CHEESE OMELET WITH RED PEPPER SAUCE

This is a warming, earthy autumn omelet. If you have a garden, use beet tops, turnip tops, or a combination of any greens you might be growing.

1 large omelet, 2 servings

1 TABLESPOON OLIVE OIL

2 SWEET RED BELL PEPPERS

1 SMALL ONION, CHOPPED

SALT AND FRESHLY GROUND PEPPER

1 TEASPOON LIGHT BROWN SUGAR (OPTIONAL)

¼ POUND PANCETTA OR BACON, CUT INTO
   ½-INCH SLICES

3 CLOVES GARLIC, FINELY MINCED

1 LARGE BUNCH COOKING GREENS OR SPINACH
   (1½ POUND), WASHED AND ROUGHLY CHOPPED

2 TABLESPOONS CHOPPED FRESH THYME

3 OUNCES GOAT CHEESE (CHÈVRE, GOAT
   RICOTTA, OR FRESH FETA)

6 EGGS, BEATEN

To make the red pepper sauce, in a large sauté pan over low heat, warm the olive oil and sauté the peppers and onion. Cover and cook, stirring occasionally, until both are very soft. Transfer to a food processor or blender and process until smooth. Season with salt and pepper and, if the sauce is bitter, add the brown sugar. Transfer to a bowl.

Preheat the oven or broiler to 400 degrees.

In the same sauté pan, cook the pancetta until slightly browned. Add the garlic, greens, and thyme. Toss thoroughly and cover with a lid. Over low heat, cook the greens until wilted, turning occasionally. Season with salt and pepper.

Increase the heat to medium. Pour the eggs into the pan over the greens. Push the edges of the omelet toward the center, tilting the pan and pushing the uncooked eggs to the outer edge. Continue until all the uncooked egg is cooked.

Dot the cheese over the omelet. Place under the broiler or in a hot oven for a few minutes, or until the eggs are cooked and the cheese is warmed. Remove the pan from the oven and using a spatula, fold the omelet in half. Slide it onto a plate.

Spoon 2 or 3 tablespoons of the red pepper sauce over the top of the omelet.

. . . .

Do Ahead: Make the red pepper sauce. Cool, cover, and refrigerate overnight. Cook the pancetta, garlic, and greens. Cool, cover, and refrigerate.

In the Morning (10 minutes): Warm the red pepper sauce and the greens. Make the omelet.

. . . .

GREEK TORTA

You can substitute a 16-ounce package of frozen spinach, thawed and squeezed dry, for the steamed spinach below.

4 to 6 servings

2 LARGE BUNCHES OF SPINACH

10 EGGS

1 CUP MILK OR SOUR CREAM

6 OUNCES FETA CHEESE, CRUMBLED

1 TEASPOON SALT

½ TEASPOON FRESHLY GROUND PEPPER

2 TABLESPOONS EXTRA-VIRGIN OLIVE OIL

1 MEDIUM RED ONION, SLICED THIN

2 GENEROUS TABLESPOONS FINELY CHOPPED FRESH OREGANO

FINELY GRATED ZEST OF 1 LEMON

¾ CUP PITTED, CHOPPED KALAMATA OLIVES

Wash the spinach thoroughly, and steam it until very soft, about 5 minutes. When cool enough to handle, squeeze out the excess liquid and chop the spinach coarsely. Set it aside.

Preheat the oven to 375 degrees.

Whisk the eggs with the milk, cheese, salt, and pepper.

Heat a heavy, ovenproof, 10-inch skillet over medium heat, and add the oil. When it's hot, sauté the onion until slightly softened, about 3 minutes. Stir in the oregano, lemon zest, and olives.

Turn the heat to high. When the oil just begins to smoke, pour in the egg mixture. Remove the pan from the heat and stir slightly to disperse the ingredients evenly.

Bake until firm in the center, about 45 minutes. Cool for at least 15 minutes. Cut it into wedges and serve it directly from the pan.

. . . .

Do Ahead: Cook, drain, and chop the spinach. Slice the onion, oregano, and olives. Grate the lemon zest. Beat together the egg mixture. Refrigerate all, covered.

In the Morning (about 1 hour): Assemble and bake the torta as directed.

. . . .

TORTA MURCIA

Murcia is a city in Spain where I once spent a glorious vacation. Hearty and flavorful, this Spanish-style torta would be wonderful served as breakfast in bed for dinner. When it's ready, light candles, crawl into bed with your partner, and end the day on a soft, intimate note.

4 to 6 servings

2 TABLESPOONS EXTRA-VIRGIN OLIVE OIL

1 MEDIUM ONION, CHOPPED

½ SWEET RED PEPPER, CHOPPED

6 OUNCES CHICKEN BREAST MEAT, CUT INTO
   BITE-SIZE PIECES

8 OUNCES SPICY PORK SAUSAGE, CUT INTO
   BITE-SIZE PIECES

1 TO 2 TABLESPOONS CHOPPED FRESH ROSEMARY

PINCH OF SAFFRON

2 TABLESPOONS DRY RED WINE, CHICKEN
   STOCK, OR WATER

10 LARGE EGGS

1½ CUPS COOKED RICE

1 TEASPOON SALT

½ TEASPOON FRESHLY GROUND PEPPER

½ CUP FINELY CHOPPED FRESH BASIL

Preheat the oven to 375 degrees.

Heat an ovenproof, 10-inch skillet over medium heat, and add the oil. When it's hot, sauté the onion, red pepper, chicken, and sausage until the vegetables are soft and the meat is completely cooked, about 10 minutes. Stir in the rosemary, saffron, and red wine, and sauté for 2 minutes more.

Meanwhile, whisk together the eggs, rice, salt, pepper, and basil.

Turn the heat under the skillet to high. When the oil just begins to smoke, pour in the egg mixture. Remove the pan from the heat and stir slightly to disperse the ingredients evenly.

Bake until firm in the center, about 45 minutes. Cool for at least 15 minutes. If the pan is well seasoned, you can invert the torta onto a platter. If not, cut it into wedges and serve it directly from the pan.

Serve leftovers for breakfast or lunch. They will keep in the refrigerator for 2 to 3 days.

. . . .

DO AHEAD: Cook the vegetable-meat mixture. Whisk together the egg mixture. Refrigerate both, covered, overnight.

IN THE MORNING (ABOUT 1 HOUR): Warm the vegetable-meat mixture in the skillet, and complete the torta.

. . . .

POTATO, ONION, AND PARSNIP FRITTATA

This frittata is a takeoff on the classic potato omelet served at tapas bars all over Spain. Incorporating the parsnips adds another level of flavor, imparting a subtle sweetness and earthiness. I like it best at room temperature with warm pita bread, whole wheat tortillas, or other flat bread.

4 to 6 servings

1 POUND WHITE OR GOLDEN-FLESHED
    POTATOES, SCRUBBED
½ POUND PARSNIPS, SCRUBBED
1 MEDIUM ONION
EXTRA-VIRGIN OLIVE OIL
LEAVES FROM 2 OR 3 SPRIGS OF FRESH THYME,
    OREGANO, OR MARJORAM
SALT AND FRESHLY GROUND PEPPER
8 LARGE EGGS, BEATEN

Slice the potatoes, parsnips, and onion into thin rounds or half circles.

Heat a heavy 10- or 12-inch skillet over medium-high heat, and add 1 tablespoon of olive oil. Just before the oil smokes, scatter a single layer of potatoes, parsnips, and onion over the bottom of the pan. Brown on both sides, and then cook, covered, until the vegetables are cooked through,

about 5 minutes. Season with fresh herbs and salt and pepper to taste, and transfer to a plate. Cook and season the rest of the vegetables in the same way, in as many batches as necessary, adding more olive oil to the pan as needed.

If you are using the oven to finish the frittata, preheat it to 400 degrees.

Generously re-oil the skillet, ladle the cooked vegetables back in, and heat over medium-high heat. Pour in the eggs, stirring slightly so that they run between the layers of vegetables. Cook until browned lightly on the bottom, about 5 minutes.

You can finish the frittata in the oven, or flip it, reduce the heat to medium-low, and finish it on the stovetop. It's done when it's firm in the center. It will take about 25 minutes in the oven and 10 minutes on top of the stove.

Let it cool for at least 15 minutes. If the pan is well seasoned, you can invert the frittata onto a platter. If not, cut it into wedges and serve it directly from the pan.

....

DO AHEAD: One option is to make the frittata from beginning to end and refrigerate it, covered. If preparing it in the morning, cut up and refrigerate the potatoes, parsnips, and herbs the night before.

IN THE MORNING (20 MINUTES TO 1 HOUR): Rewarm the frittata in a 400-degree oven for about 15 minutes. Or cook it from the beginning as directed.

....

ASPARAGUS, SUN-DRIED TOMATO, WILD RICE, AND SPRING GARLIC FRITTATA

As winter ends and the first shoots of asparagus and tender green garlic are sold in my farmer's market, I celebrate by sitting down to this lovely breakfast. Sometimes I double the recipe and send leftovers off in a bag lunch with someone I love— a small reminder that, through food, I can touch him from afar and show that I care.

2 servings

4 OR 5 SUN-DRIED TOMATOES

3 OR 4 MEDIUM STALKS ASPARAGUS, TRIMMED AND COOKED

2 OR 3 WHOLE SPRIGS SPRING GARLIC OR GREEN ONIONS

5 EGGS

SALT AND FRESHLY GROUND PEPPER

1 TABLESPOON LIGHT OLIVE OIL

2 TABLESPOONS COOKED WILD RICE

2 TABLESPOONS CHOPPED FRESH THYME

2 TABLESPOONS CHOPPED FRESH PARSLEY

3 OUNCES FETA CHEESE, CRUMBLED

Rehydrate the tomatoes in hot water to cover for about 5 minutes; drain and chop them. Cut the asparagus into 1-inch pieces. Slice the spring garlic into thin rounds. Beat the eggs with salt and pepper to taste.

Heat a heavy, 10-inch skillet over medium heat, and add the olive oil. When it's hot, stir in the vegetables, rice, and herbs. Pour the beaten eggs over all. Using a wooden spoon or spatula, scramble them gently until almost cooked. Sprinkle on the cheese, and let the eggs finish cooking without stirring so that a brown crust forms on the bottom and sides.

If you can, flip the frittata over and brown the other side. If not, cover the pan, remove it from the burner, and let it sit until the cheese melts, about 2 minutes.

Cut the frittata into wedges and serve.

....

DO AHEAD: Prepare the vegetables and herbs, mix them with the wild rice, and refrigerate, covered.

IN THE MORNING (ABOUT 20 MINUTES): Heat the vegetable mixture in the olive oil, and cook the frittata as directed.

....

APPLE, HAM, SAGE DERBY, AND CHIVE FRITTATA

Sage Derby is similar to an English Cheddar that is laced with the scent of musty sage. You'll find it at a good cheese shop; if you can't, substitute aged Cheddar and a generous pinch of dried sage. Combined with apple and ham, it will have your lucky breakfast guest begging to stay in bed and have seconds.

2 servings

2 TEASPOONS UNSALTED BUTTER OR VEGETABLE OIL

1 TART APPLE, PEELED, CORED, AND SLICED THIN

4 OUNCES HAM, CHOPPED

4 OR 5 LARGE EGGS

2 TO 4 TABLESPOONS CHOPPED CHIVES OR GREEN ONIONS

FRESHLY GROUND PEPPER

4 TO 6 OUNCES SAGE DERBY, CRUMBLED

Melt the butter in a heavy, medium-size skillet over medium heat. Sauté the apple slices and ham for 2 or 3 minutes, until slightly softened.

Beat the eggs with the chives and pepper to taste, and pour them into the pan. Using a spatula or wooden spoon, scramble the eggs gently until almost cooked. Stir in the cheese. Let the eggs finish cooking without stirring so that a brown crust forms on the bottom and sides.

If you can, flip the frittata over and brown the other side. If not, cover the pan, remove it from the burner, and let it sit until the cheese melts, about 2 minutes. Cut into wedges and serve.

. . . .

DO AHEAD: Prepare and sauté the apples and ham. Chop the chives. Crumble the cheese. Refrigerate all, covered.

IN THE MORNING (ABOUT 10 MINUTES): Warm the apple mixture in the skillet, and cook the frittata as directed.

. . . .

SMOKED WHITEFISH, RED ONION, AND CAPER FRITTATA WITH CAVIAR-CHIVE SOUR CREAM

This frittata is guaranteed to get the attention of the one you love when you want some snuggling and he or she seems content to read the Sunday paper.

2 TABLESPOONS SOUR CREAM

2 TEASPOONS CHOPPED FRESH CHIVES

1 TABLESPOON DRY VERMOUTH

6 TO 8 OUNCES SMOKED WHITEFISH

UNSALTED BUTTER OR VEGETABLE OIL

1 SMALL RED ONION, CHOPPED FINE

2 TEASPOONS CAPERS

5 OR 6 EGGS, BEATEN

2 OR MORE TEASPOONS CAVIAR

CHIVES OR CHIVE BLOSSOMS FOR GARNISH

Mix the sour cream, chives, and vermouth in a small bowl, and set aside.

Remove the skin and bones from the fish, and flake the flesh into large bite-size pieces. Set aside.

Melt 1 or 2 tablespoons of butter in a heavy, medium-size skillet over medium heat. (If you have a nonstick pan you'll need less.) Sauté the onion until soft, about 5 minutes.

If using the broiler to finish the frittata, preheat it.

Add the fish, capers, and beaten eggs to the onion. Using a spatula or wooden spoon, scramble the eggs gently until almost cooked. Let them finish cooking without stirring so that a brown crust forms on the bottom and sides. If you can, flip the frittata over and brown the other side. If not, put it under the broiler or in a hot oven until lightly browned, about 10 minutes.

Invert the frittata onto a serving platter if you can, or cut it in wedges and serve it directly from the pan. Garnish with the sour cream mixture, caviar, and chopped chives or chive blossoms.

....

DO AHEAD: Prepare the sour cream mixture and the fish, and chop the onion. Refrigerate all, covered.

IN THE MORNING (ABOUT 20 MINUTES): Cook and garnish the frittata as directed.

....

FRESH CORN AND BACON PUDDING (PAGE 58)

Spoon Foods

Steaming cereals or cooling grains, fruit, and yogurt are expected breakfast meals in a bowl. Yet soups and stews—spicy harissa in Morocco, rich, brown miso soup in Japan, or a simple stew of meat and potatoes left over from your own dinner table—can be a warming and nurturing way to welcome the day. There is something grounding about having a bowl full of flavorful food nestled in one hand, spoon poised in the other, awaiting the plunge.

Maybe that's why I prefer soup for breakfast over just about anything else. I eat a giant bowl of soup or broth for breakfast three or four times a week, hot weather or cold. If you think your schedule is too hectic to accommodate soup mak-

ing, do what I do and put a big batch of vegetable or chicken stock on to cook in your Crock-Pot whenever you have the chance. The long, slow cooking produces the deepest, most old-fashioned flavors and the most wonderfully nurturing aromas. (At times like that I think of that Crock-Pot as my personal wife and mother!) Stash the extra stock in the freezer, and you'll be ready to make a seasonal pot of soup—potato, spinach, leek, or asparagus in spring, minestrone in summer, cabbage or beet in fall, and hearty root vegetables in winter.

Whether you're serving soup, porridge, or bread pudding for breakfast, the choice of bowl is important. Traditional shallow ones can be hard to maneuver in bed and are best left on the table. You need something that can be lifted to the mouth, even slurped from, easily grasped while digging in with a spoon. Those giant mugs with big handles, sold for coffee, are my favorite breakfast bowls, great for cereal, soups, anything spoonable.

And then there's the spoon. I like to choose my bites carefully, getting a bit of everything with each one. For that, the spoon must be oversized, well weighted, with good concave lines. If you are a small-bite person, by all means choose a small spoon, but choose thoughtfully.

In warmer weather, nothing is lovelier for breakfast than a big bowl of seasonal berries topped with a sprinkle of granola or matched with a home-baked muffin. Leftover rice finds its way into my bowl, sprinkled with sugar and milk and memories of a dish my father ate often. Bread puddings, grits, and polenta, too—if you can serve it in a bowl, call it breakfast and dig in.

CHICKEN BROTH WITH TOASTED BREAD AND ITALIAN CHEESE

Eating broth over a thick slice of bread is something my Italian grandfather did. For Papa, the comfort of so warming a dish, always eaten with an oversized soup spoon, brought back memories of his parents in the old country.

Use free-range, hormone-free chicken if possible, and try to include some smoked chicken or bones; they add an addictive richness to the stock. A full-flavored fresh chicken, vegetable, beef, or ham-bone stock is good served this way, too.

2 servings

FOR THE BROTH

2 POUNDS CHICKEN BONES AND PARTS (NECKS, WINGS, BACKS), SOME SMOKED IF POSSIBLE

1 LARGE ONION, CUT INTO WEDGES

2 GARLIC CLOVES, CRUSHED

1 CARROT, CUT INTO ½-INCH SLICES

4 SPRIGS PARSLEY OR FRESH FENNEL LEAVES

5 PEPPERCORNS

2 QUARTS COLD WATER

SALT

TO FINISH THE DISH

2 THICK SLICES SOURDOUGH BREAD

3 TO 4 OUNCES GRATED ASIAGO, AGED PROVOLONE, OR OTHER FLAVORFUL DRIED ITALIAN CHEESE

CHOPPED PARSLEY FOR GARNISH

Preheat the oven to 400 degrees.

Spread the chicken bones and parts on a baking sheet, and bake until nicely browned, about 30 minutes.

TO MAKE THE BROTH

Put the chicken in a large stockpot with the onion, garlic, carrot, parsley, and peppercorns, and cover with 2 quarts of cold water. Bring to a gentle simmer over medium-high heat. Reduce the heat to a simmer; cook for 2 to 3 hours, until reduced by about half. Sometimes I let it simmer overnight in a Crock-Pot, and the aroma awakens me far more pleasantly than any alarm clock.

Strain the broth through a colander, reserving the onion and carrot if you choose. Season to taste with salt, and refrigerate overnight. Remove the fat that floats to the top.

TO FINISH THE DISH

Reheat the stock. Toast the bread in a well-seasoned skillet or under the broiler until golden brown on both sides. Put each piece in a shallow soup bowl, and top it with reserved carrot and onion if you like. Pour on hot stock to cover the bread halfway. Sprinkle on the grated cheese and chopped parsley, and serve.

. . . .

DO AHEAD: Make the broth. Chop the parsley and grate the cheese.

IN THE MORNING (ABOUT 10 MINUTES): Heat the broth, toast the bread, and assemble the dish.

. . . .

COMFORTING RICE WITH MILK, SUGAR, AND BUTTER

My dad loved this simple dish, similar to rice pudding, and eating it brings back memories of feeling loved by him. Use leftover brown, basmati, or regular white rice, and white, date, brown, or turbinado sugar, or even maple syrup, to sweeten it.

2 servings

2 CUPS COOKED RICE

½ TO ⅔ CUP COLD MILK

BUTTER

SUGAR

A GRATING OF NUTMEG (OPTIONAL)

⅛ TEASPOON VANILLA EXTRACT (OPTIONAL)

In a small saucepan over medium heat, warm the rice with ¼ cup of the milk until steaming. Spoon it into two bowls, dab it with butter, and sprinkle it with sugar to taste. Pour on the remaining cold milk, grate on nutmeg and add a bit of vanilla if you like, and serve.

. . . .

DO AHEAD: Cook the rice.

IN THE MORNING (ABOUT 5 MINUTES): Warm the rice and milk, and serve as directed.

. . . .

OAT PORRIDGE

Nourishing, rib-sticking porridge is meant to be thick and well cooked. It's done when a spoon will stand straight up in the middle of the pot. The texture of the porridge is not quite the same when it's cooked ahead and reheated, but if getting back to bed with a loved one is the objective, this is the way to go. I prefer old-fashioned organic oats or Irish oatmeal.

2 servings

2 CUPS WATER OR MILK

⅔ CUP ROLLED OATS

PINCH OF SALT

GROUND CINNAMON (OPTIONAL)

Bring the water to a boil in a saucepan. Stir in the oats and salt, and reduce the heat to a simmer. Cook, uncovered, stirring occasionally, until the porridge is thick, about 20 minutes. Serve in bowls with milk and a sprinkling of cinnamon if you like.

....

DO AHEAD: Cook the porridge and refrigerate, covered, overnight.

IN THE MORNING (ABOUT 10 MINUTES): Thin the porridge with a bit of milk or water and reheat it in a heavy saucepan, stirring, over medium-low heat, until steaming.

....

TOASTED WHEAT BERRIES WITH MILK AND HONEY

A bowl of wheat berries is a perfect source of vitamin B and natural fiber. Look for already-toasted wheat berries at your natural foods store. Or toast your own in a skillet over medium heat until they pop and give off a toasty aroma.

4 to 6 servings

3 CUPS WATER

1 CUP TOASTED WHEAT BERRIES

SALT

CINNAMON

VANILLA OR ALMOND EXTRACT

MILK

HONEY OR SUGAR

Bring the water to a boil in a 3-quart saucepan. Stir in the wheat berries, reduce the heat to a simmer, and cook, covered, until soft, about 1 hour. Drain off any water; season with salt to taste and a touch of cinnamon and vanilla. Serve with milk and honey.

....

DO AHEAD: Cook the wheat berries and refrigerate, covered.

IN THE MORNING: Reheat the wheat berries in a saucepan over medium-low heat, thinning them with a little water if necessary, and serve.

....

SPOON BREAD WITH ANDOUILLE SAUSAGE AND BAKED EGGS

Spoon bread is like a rich, dense pudding. Sausage and eggs add wonderful depth and texture to this version. For even more flavor, top it with melted chipotle butter (page 97).

2 servings

1 CUP WATER

½ TEASPOON SALT

1 TEASPOON BROWN SUGAR

½ CUP COARSE WHITE, YELLOW, OR BLUE CORNMEAL

4 EGGS

4 TABLESPOONS BUTTER

½ CUP WHOLE MILK

4 OUNCES ANDOUILLE SMOKED CHICKEN SAUSAGE, CHOPPED INTO ½-INCH PIECES

2 GREEN ONIONS, SLICED THIN

1 TEASPOON BAKING POWDER

2 TABLESPOONS CHOPPED FRESH BASIL, OREGANO, MARJORAM, OR THYME

½ TEASPOON DRIED RED PEPPER FLAKES

Bring the water, salt, and brown sugar to a boil in a saucepan. Gradually whisk in the cornmeal. Reduce the heat to a simmer and cook, uncovered, stirring frequently, until thickened, about 20 minutes.

While the cornmeal is cooking, separate two of the eggs. Whip the whites until stiff, and beat the yolks.

Preheat the oven to 375 degrees. Generously grease a 1-quart baking dish or two 1½-cup ramekins with 1 tablespoon of the butter.

When the cornmeal is thick, stir in the rest of the butter until melted. Stir in the milk, egg yolks, sausage, and onions until well blended. Let the mixture cool for 15 minutes. Stir in the baking powder, fresh herbs, and pepper flakes. Fold in the egg whites, one-third at a time.

Spread half the batter into the prepared baking dish or ramekins. If using ramekins, crack one egg in the center of each one. If using the baking dish, crack both eggs near the center. Spread the remaining batter over the eggs but don't cover them completely.

Bake until the egg whites are firm and the yolks are cooked, 35 to 40 minutes for the large dish and 20 to 25 minutes for the individual ones. Serve hot.

OLD-FASHIONED BREAD AND BUTTER PUDDING

You probably think of bread pudding as dessert, but it can be a sweet, luscious way to start the day, too. This version has lots of custard—the best part of bread pudding, if you ask me. Reheat any leftovers for dessert.

4 to 6 servings

6 THICK SLICES OF WHITE BREAD

4 TABLESPOONS UNSALTED BUTTER, SOFTENED

8 EGG YOLKS

1¼ CUPS SUGAR

2 TEASPOONS VANILLA EXTRACT

2 TEASPOONS CINNAMON

3½ CUPS WHOLE MILK

Preheat the oven to 350 degrees.

Spread both sides of the bread with butter, and lay it in a deep-sided, 2-quart baking dish.

Whisk together the egg yolks, sugar, vanilla, cinnamon, and milk, and pour over the bread.

Set the baking dish in a larger pan and put it in the oven. Pour enough hot water into the pan to come halfway up the sides of the baking dish. Bake until the custard is firm in the center, about 45 minutes. Let it cool for 15 minutes before serving.

DO AHEAD: Bake the bread pudding and refrigerate, covered.

IN THE MORNING (ABOUT 20 MINUTES): Reheat the pudding in a 375-degree oven for about 20 minutes.

FRESH CORN AND BACON PUDDING

This corn custard was one of the first dishes my son Jonah ever made for me. He made so much that we ended up having leftovers for breakfast the next day, and decided it was fantastic with a drizzle of maple syrup.

2 servings

2 CUPS FRESH CORN KERNELS

1½ CUPS MILK

2 TABLESPOONS UNSALTED BUTTER PLUS MORE FOR THE PAN

2 TABLESPOONS UNBLEACHED WHITE FLOUR

2 EGGS, BEATEN

½ TEASPOON SALT

¼ TEASPOON FRESHLY GROUND PEPPER

3 SLICES THICK BACON, FRIED CRISP AND CRUMBLED

½ CUP GRATED CHEDDAR CHEESE (OPTIONAL)

CHOPPED GREEN ONIONS FOR GARNISH

Soak the corn in the milk for 15 minutes.

Preheat the oven to 350 degrees. Generously butter a 1-quart baking dish.

Melt the 2 tablespoons of butter in a saucepan over medium heat. Whisk in the flour, and cook it for 2 or 3 minutes, stirring.

Drain the corn, and whisk the milk into the flour mixture. Simmer it until slightly thickened, about 5 minutes.

Remove the pan from the heat and whisk in the eggs. Stir in the corn, salt, pepper, and bacon.

Pour the corn mixture into the prepared pan, and sprinkle the cheese on top. Bake it until brown on top and firm to the touch, about 45 minutes. Let it cool for 10 minutes before spooning it into bowls and topping it with green onions.

. . . .

DO AHEAD: Make the corn pudding and refrigerate it. It loses some of its lightness and velvety texture, but my son maintains that the flavor improves. Chop the green onions.

IN THE MORNING (ABOUT 25 MINUTES): Warm the pudding in a 375-degree oven for about 20 minutes. Spoon into shallow bowls or small plates, garnish, and serve.

. . . .

DEEP-DISH VEGETABLE POT PIE

With a little foresight, this savory dish can come together in 15 minutes and be on the table in 45 minutes. The trick is to make, roll, and freeze the pie dough well in advance.

4 servings

YOUR FAVORITE DOUGH FOR A 9-INCH SINGLE-CRUST PIE

1 TABLESPOON LIGHT OLIVE OIL

½ SMALL ONION, CHOPPED FINE

½ CUP SLICED MUSHROOMS

2 TABLESPOONS COOKING SHERRY

3 TABLESPOONS BUTTER

3 TABLESPOONS UNBLEACHED WHITE FLOUR

1 CUP VEGETABLE STOCK OR MILK

2 CUPS COOKED VEGETABLES (CARROTS, PEAS, POTATOES, RUTABAGAS, PARSNIPS, GREENS)

SALT AND FRESHLY GROUND PEPPER

FRESHLY GRATED NUTMEG

¾ CUP GRATED CHEDDAR CHEESE (OPTIONAL)

Roll the dough to ¼-inch thickness, and cut it into four rounds the size of the ramekins you will be using. I suggest dishes about 4 inches across and 4 inches deep. Layer the pastry rounds between pieces of parchment or waxed paper, and refrigerate or freeze them until needed.

(continued)

Heat a saucepan over medium heat, and add the oil. When it's hot, sauté the onion and mushrooms until soft, about 5 minutes. Raise the heat to medium-high, stir in the sherry, and cook 2 minutes longer. Using a slotted spoon, transfer the onions and mushrooms to a bowl, leaving the oil and juices behind.

Melt the butter in the same pan over medium heat, and whisk in the flour. Cook for about 3 minutes, whisking frequently. Slowly pour in the stock, whisking constantly. Cook until very thick, about 5 minutes.

Remove the pan from the heat, and stir in the mushrooms, onions, cooked vegetables, and salt, pepper, and nutmeg to taste.

Preheat the oven to 375 degrees.

Spoon the filling into four ramekins, and sprinkle with grated cheese if you choose. Top each one with a pastry round.

Bake for 20 to 25 minutes, until the crust is golden brown and the filling is hot. Serve immediately.

. . . .

Do Ahead: Make, roll, and cut the pie dough; refrigerate or freeze it. Grate the cheese, cook the filling, and refrigerate.

In the Morning (about 35 minutes): Thaw the dough. Heat the filling to room temperature. (If it's too hot, it will melt the butter in the pastry dough.) Assemble and bake the pot pies as directed.

. . . .

POLENTA WITH MAPLE SYRUP AND MASCARPONE

Polenta was a staple in my Italian grandparents' house. My grandmother often made it with milk and usually cooked it for hours, making it thick, rich, and creamy. For breakfast, we got steaming bowls of this lovely cornmeal mush topped with real maple syrup and a spoonful of soft cream cheese. This is my version of that treasured dish.

6 to 8 servings

6 cups water, milk, or stock
2 cups cornmeal
1 tablespoon salt
Maple syrup
Mascarpone or sour cream

Bring the water to a boil in a large saucepan. Working quickly, whisk in the cornmeal and salt, and reduce the heat to a simmer. Cook, uncovered, stirring frequently, until thick and velvety, at least 45 minutes. If the polenta is too thin, cook it longer. If it is thick but not smooth, add more water and continue cooking. You cannot overcook polenta.

Spoon it into bowls and top it with generous drizzles of maple syrup and dollops of mascarpone.

Pour leftovers into a well-oiled pan. It will keep in the refrigerator for 3 or 4 days. Slice and bake, grill, or panfry for breakfast or a dinner side dish.

. . . .

DO AHEAD: Soft polenta must be served fresh cooked; it easily becomes lumpy if reheated. It is surprising, though, how much time is saved by doing a few things ahead: Measure out the cornmeal and water, and have the salt and any toppings at hand.

IN THE MORNING (ABOUT 50 MINUTES): Crawl out of bed and get the polenta cooking while the coffee brews. Garnish and serve it as directed.

. . . .

HOMINY GRITS WITH PEPPERS, CAJUN SHRIMP, AND BASTED EGGS

The simplicity and bone-hugging goodness of old-fashioned grits bring back memories of breakfasts devoured in small-town diners while traveling through the South in 1974. Hominy grits are ground dried white or yellow corn. Though there are instant and quick-cooking grits on the market, there is no substitute for the slower-cooking kind, which actually takes only about 30 minutes from beginning to end.

2 generous servings

2½ CUPS WATER

1 TO 1½ TEASPOONS SALT

½ CUP HOMINY GRITS

1 TABLESPOON OLIVE OIL

¼ CUP CHOPPED YELLOW ONION

¼ CUP CHOPPED GREEN BELL PEPPER

2 GARLIC CLOVES, CHOPPED

1 TABLESPOON CHOPPED FRESH THYME

½ TEASPOON PAPRIKA

CAYENNE

½ CUP CHICKEN STOCK OR WATER

½ POUND PEELED AND DEVEINED SHRIMP

4 EGGS

CHOPPED PARSLEY OR CHIVES FOR GARNISH

Bring the water to a boil in a 3-quart saucepan. Working quickly, whisk in the salt and grits. Reduce the heat to a simmer. Cook, uncovered, stirring frequently, until thick and creamy, about 30 minutes.

Meanwhile, heat a skillet over medium heat, and add the oil. When it's hot, sauté the onion, bell pepper, and garlic until soft, about 5 minutes. Stir in the thyme, paprika, cayenne to taste, and the chicken stock and bring to a simmer. Reduce the heat, cover, and cook for about 5 minutes. Set aside off the heat.

When the grits are nearly cooked, return the vegetables to the stove over medium heat. Add the shrimp and simmer for 3 or 4 minutes, until they curl slightly and become opaque. Crack the eggs into the pan, ladle pan juices over them, and cook, covered, for a few minutes, until they're done to your liking.

Spoon the grits into two bowls, pressing down to make an indentation in the center of each one. Nestle a basted egg in the grits, and top with the shrimp mixture. Garnish with parsley and serve.

. . . .

Do Ahead: Cook the vegetable mixture. Measure and set out the ingredients for the grits.

In the Morning (about 40 minutes): Cook the grits. Reheat the vegetable mixture, and cook the shrimp and eggs as directed.

. . . .

GRITS WITH BRIE, GREEN GARLIC, AND ASPARAGUS

When the weather begins to turn warm after a long winter, the first asparagus and green garlic bring this simple yet luxurious dish to mind. Try it with rye or buckwheat grits if you can find them in your natural foods store, and adjust the cooking time according to the package directions.

2 servings

2½ CUPS WATER OR MILK

½ CUP HOMINY GRITS

1½ TEASPOONS SALT

4 STALKS ASPARAGUS, COOKED AND CUT INTO
   1-INCH PIECES

2 GREEN GARLIC SHOOTS OR GREEN ONIONS,
   TENDER PART ONLY, CHOPPED FINE

3 OUNCES BRIE OR MILD GOAT CHEESE, CUT
   INTO BITE-SIZE PIECES

ROSE PETALS AND CHOPPED SAGE FOR
   GARNISH (OPTIONAL)

Bring the water to a boil in a 3-quart saucepan. Working quickly, whisk in the grits and salt. Reduce the heat to a simmer. Cook, uncovered, stirring frequently, until thick and creamy, about 30 minutes.

Divide the asparagus and garlic shoots into two bowls. Spoon the cooked grits on top. Push the bits of Brie into the grits, and garnish with rose petals and sage if you choose.

. . . .

Do Ahead: Measure out the water, grits, and salt, and store covered. Cook and slice the asparagus, and cut up the green garlic and Brie; refrigerate all, covered.

In the Morning (about 40 minutes): Cook the grits and assemble the dish as directed.

. . . .

FIG AND GOAT CHEESE PUDDING
WITH RASPBERRIES

Make this luscious pudding at the end of the summer when figs and raspberries are at their prime. Serve it with grilled whole wheat bread and tall glasses of freshly squeezed orange juice or as a dessert after dinner.

4 servings

8 OUNCES SOFT GOAT CHEESE (CHÈVRE)

4 OUNCES RICOTTA CHEESE

4 LARGE EGGS

½ CUP WHITE OR RAW SUGAR

1 TEASPOON VANILLA EXTRACT

FINELY GRATED ZEST OF 1 LEMON

1 PINT FRESH MISSION FIGS, CUT IN HALVES OR QUARTERS

½ PINT RASPBERRIES OR BLACKBERRIES

FRESHLY GRATED NUTMEG

Preheat the oven to 350 degrees. Butter a 1½-quart baking dish.

Beat the goat cheese and ricotta with an electric mixer on medium speed. Reduce the speed to low and beat in the eggs one at a time. Add the sugar, vanilla, and lemon zest. Increase the speed to medium and beat until smooth.

Spread the batter in the prepared pan. Arrange the figs on top, and press down to submerge them halfway. Bake the pudding until slightly firm in the center, about 25 minutes.

Let the pudding cool for 30 minutes before serving. Spoon it into bowls, and garnish each one with a generous handful of raspberries and a grating of nutmeg.

....

DO AHEAD: Bake the pudding and refrigerate it, covered.

IN THE MORNING (ABOUT 15 MINUTES): Reheat the pudding in a 375-degree oven for about 10 minutes.

....

BUTTERMILK-PECAN WAFFLES (PAGE 77)

Pancakes and Waffles

There's nothing more grounding than a plate of piping hot griddle cakes drenched in real maple syrup or a steaming waffle smothered in mushroom gravy. Around my house, waffles and pancakes are mainly for breakfast, but every now and then, my kids beg to have "breakfast for dinner." That means an early dinner of pancakes, waffles, eggs, toast, sausage, and potatoes—you know, the works.

Pancakes and waffles are great filler-uppers and energy food, an inexpensive and popular choice for my teenage son and his friends. I like to make a batch for the famished bunch of them after they have spent the night on my living room floor watching movies. When the batter is coming together, one of the guys usually finds his way into the kitchen, and is amazed to see how quickly pancakes or waffles can be made from scratch rather than from a mix. I'd like to imagine some of these boys finding joy in making the same kind of breakfast for their own kids someday.

Many pancake and waffle batters can be prepared the night before (refer to the Do Ahead for each recipe). Store it in an airtight container in the refrigerator. Should discoloring occur on the surface, ignore it or scrape it off. For best results, those that have beaten egg whites are best finished in the morning. In a pinch, these batters can be prepared entirely the night before but will produce a slightly heavier pancake or waffle.

By making the batter in advance or following the Do-Ahead tips in each chapter, you can embrace the basic philosophy of this book, which is to get yourself back in bed, eating breakfast or otherwise, within about a half hour.

BANANA PANCAKES

Sometimes I stir the bananas right into the batter; other times I cook slices of them on top of these lovely pancakes as below. Use all unbleached white flour for lighter pancakes and 1¼ cups unbleached white and ¾ cup whole wheat for heartier, earthier-tasting ones.

2 generous servings

2 CUPS FLOUR (SEE ABOVE)

1 TEASPOON BAKING SODA

½ TEASPOON SALT

2 EGGS, LIGHTLY BEATEN

2½ CUPS BUTTERMILK

1 TEASPOON VANILLA EXTRACT

3 TABLESPOONS VEGETABLE OIL OR
  MELTED BUTTER

1 OR 2 RIPE BANANAS

MAPLE SYRUP, HONEY, YOGURT, OR
  SOUR CREAM

Sift the flour with the baking soda and salt into a large bowl.

In a medium bowl, whisk together the eggs, buttermilk, vanilla, and vegetable oil.

Very gradually add the liquid to the dry ingredients, mixing just until combined. Do not overmix or the pancakes will be tough.

Peel and thinly slice the bananas. (If you'd rather garnish the finished pancakes with bananas, wait to slice them.)

Heat a griddle or heavy skillet over medium heat, and lightly grease it with vegetable oil. Preheat the oven to 250 degrees.

Drop heaping tablespoonfuls of batter into the hot pan. When the tops of the pancakes begin to bubble, cover them with banana slices. When the pancakes are lightly browned on the bottom, flip them. As they cook through, transfer them to a baking sheet and keep them warm in the oven while you cook the rest of the batter.

Serve warm with maple syrup, honey, yogurt, or sour cream.

．．．．．．．．．．．．．．．．．．．．．．．．．．．．．．．．．．．．．

DO AHEAD: The batter can be prepared entirely the night before. Or stir together the dry ingredients and store at room temperature. Whisk together the wet ingredients and refrigerate, covered, overnight.

IN THE MORNING (ABOUT 15 MINUTES): Heat the griddle. Stir together the batter, slice the bananas, and cook the pancakes.

．．．．．．．．．．．．．．．．．．．．．．．．．．．．．．．．．．．．．

OAT PANCAKES

Serve these hearty pancakes with yogurt and real maple syrup.

4 servings

1 CUP OLD-FASHIONED ROLLED OATS

2 CUPS BOILING WATER

2 EGGS, BEATEN

1 TEASPOON VANILLA EXTRACT

1¼ CUPS BUTTERMILK

1 CUP UNBLEACHED WHITE OR WHOLE WHEAT FLOUR

1½ TEASPOONS BAKING SODA

½ TEASPOON SALT

1 TEASPOON GROUND CINNAMON

5 TABLESPOONS BUTTER, MELTED

VEGETABLE OIL

Stir the oats into the boiling water and set aside off the heat, covered, for 10 minutes.

Scrape the oats and water into a large bowl, and let them cool for 10 minutes. Whisk in the eggs, vanilla, and buttermilk.

In another bowl, stir together the flour, baking soda, salt, and cinnamon.

Gradually mix the dry ingredients and then the melted butter into the oat mixture, stirring just until blended. Do not overmix.

Heat a griddle or heavy skillet over medium heat, and lightly grease it with vegetable oil. Preheat the oven to 250 degrees.

Ladle the batter into the hot pan (it will be a little runny). When the pancakes are bubbly on top and nicely browned on the bottom, flip them. As they cook through, transfer them to a baking sheet and keep them warm in the oven while you cook the rest of the batter.

. . . .

DO AHEAD: Cover the oats with the hot water; when cooled, cover and refrigerate. Whisk together and refrigerate the other wet ingredients. Stir together the dry ingredients and store at room temperature. This recipe is best done in this manner and finished in the morning.

IN THE MORNING (ABOUT 15 MINUTES): Melt the butter and let it cool slightly. Warm the oat mixture on the stove or in the microwave, and thin it to a stirrable consistency with a little water. Whisk the butter and oats with the rest of the wet ingredients, and combine with the dry ingredients. Heat the griddle and cook the pancakes as directed.

. . . .

RICOTTA–COTTAGE CHEESE PANCAKES

I find myself wanting to eat too many of these moist, delicate pancakes. Topped with fruit, especially bananas, fresh berries, or juicy sliced peaches, they're a healthy, substantial way to start the day.

2 generous or 4 moderate servings

1 CUP UNBLEACHED WHITE FLOUR

1 TABLESPOON SUGAR

½ TEASPOON SALT

1 TEASPOON BAKING POWDER

4 EGGS

1 CUP RICOTTA CHEESE

1 CUP SMALL CURD COTTAGE CHEESE

¾ CUP MILK

1 TEASPOON VANILLA EXTRACT

VEGETABLE OIL

In a medium bowl, stir together the flour, sugar, salt, and baking powder.

In another bowl, beat the eggs with the ricotta, cottage cheese, milk, and vanilla.

Gradually add the wet ingredients to the dry, stirring just until blended. Do not overmix.

Heat a griddle or heavy skillet over medium heat, and lightly grease it with vegetable oil. Preheat the oven to 250 degrees.

Drop the batter onto the hot pan by heaping tablespoonfuls. When the pancakes are bubbly on top and nicely browned on the bottom, flip them. As they cook through, transfer them to a baking sheet and keep them warm in the oven while you cook the rest of the batter.

DO AHEAD: The batter can be prepared entirely the night before. Or stir together the dry ingredients and store at room temperature. Whisk together the wet ingredients and refrigerate, covered.

IN THE MORNING (ABOUT 15 MINUTES): Heat the griddle. Stir together the batter, and cook the pancakes.

GERMAN-STYLE PUFF PANCAKE WITH BERRIES

My older boy, Joshua, got this recipe in a cooking class in elementary school, and made it again and again as a treat when he wanted to be good to his mom. It doesn't quite fit with the 1990s fat- and sugar-consciousness, but it's a memorable treat, especially topped with lots of fresh berries and mint sprigs straight from the garden for a special Sunday brunch.

2 generous servings

(continued)

5 EGGS, SEPARATED

2 TABLESPOONS SUGAR

2 TABLESPOONS UNBLEACHED WHITE FLOUR

½ TEASPOON SALT

½ CUP MILK

1 TEASPOON VANILLA EXTRACT

4 TABLESPOONS UNSALTED BUTTER

CONFECTIONERS' SUGAR

FRESH BERRIES, MAPLE SYRUP, OR HONEY

   (OPTIONAL)

Preheat the oven to 450 degrees.

Whip the egg whites with an electric or hand mixer until they hold soft peaks.

In another bowl, beat the egg yolks, and whisk in the sugar, flour, salt, milk, and vanilla just until smooth.

Fold the egg whites into the egg yolk mixture.

Melt the butter in a well-seasoned 10-inch iron skillet or omelet pan over medium heat.

Pour the batter into the pan, and bake for about 10 minutes, until it puffs up.

Slide the pancake onto a big platter. Sprinkle it with confectioners' sugar, and serve it with berries, maple syrup, or honey if you choose.

....

DO AHEAD: Separate the eggs. Put the whites in one bowl; beat the yolks with the sugar, flour, salt, milk, and vanilla in another. Refrigerate, covered.

This recipe is best done in this manner and finished in the morning.

IN THE MORNING (ABOUT 20 MINUTES): Preheat the oven. Beat the egg whites, mix together the batter, and cook the pancake as directed.

....

WINTER SQUASH PANCAKES

These pancakes are a wonderful match for smoked meats. They're a natural with real maple syrup, yogurt, or sour cream, but I also like them with caramelized onions, bits of bacon, and crème fraîche.

4 servings

2 CUPS MASHED COOKED WINTER SQUASH OR

   PUMPKIN

2 TABLESPOONS BROWN SUGAR

1 CUP MILK OR APPLE JUICE

2 WHOLE EGGS, BEATEN

½ CUP UNBLEACHED WHITE FLOUR

1 TEASPOON BAKING POWDER

½ TEASPOON SALT

PINCH OF FRESHLY GRATED NUTMEG

2 TABLESPOONS CHOPPED FRESH CHIVES

   (OPTIONAL)

VEGETABLE OIL OR BUTTER

In a large bowl, beat the squash with the brown sugar, milk, and eggs until smooth.

In another bowl, stir together the flour, baking powder, salt, and nutmeg.

Stir the dry ingredients into the wet just until combined, and fold in the chives.

Heat a griddle or heavy skillet over medium heat, and lightly grease it with vegetable oil. Preheat the oven to 250 degrees.

Drop the batter onto the hot pan by heaping tablespoonfuls. Lightly oil a spatula and flatten the pancakes. When they are golden brown on the bottom, flip them. As they brown on the other side, transfer them to a baking sheet and keep them warm in the oven while you cook the rest of the batter.

. . . .

DO AHEAD: The batter can be prepared entirely the night before. Or stir together the dry ingredients and store at room temperature. Whisk together the wet ingredients and refrigerate, covered.

IN THE MORNING (ABOUT 15 MINUTES): Heat the griddle, mix the batter, and cook the pancakes.

. . . .

BUCKWHEAT-HERB BLINIS WITH CAVIAR, SOUR CREAM, AND CHIVE BLOSSOMS

These blinis must be started the night before, but you can have them ready in minutes the next morning. Cook up a batch, pop the cork on a good bottle of champagne, and seduce your lover into playing hooky from work with you some weekday morning.

2 servings

1½ TEASPOONS ACTIVE DRY YEAST

¼ CUP WARM WATER

1 CUP MILK

1½ CUPS BUCKWHEAT FLOUR

½ CUP UNBLEACHED WHITE FLOUR

2 EGGS

½ TEASPOON SALT

1 TEASPOON BAKING SODA

1 TABLESPOON BROWN SUGAR

2 TABLESPOONS CHOPPED FRESH BASIL, THYME, DILL, OR TARRAGON

3 TABLESPOONS MELTED BUTTER

VEGETABLE OIL

2 TABLESPOONS SOUR CREAM

2 TABLESPOONS CAVIAR

2 OUNCES SMOKED SALMON

CHOPPED CHIVE BLOSSOMS OR CHIVES

(continued)

Mix the yeast with the warm water, and set it aside until bubbly, about 5 minutes. Scald the milk, let it cool to room temperature, and stir it into the yeast mixture with the flours until smooth. Cover and let it stand overnight to form a sponge.

In the morning, beat the eggs with the salt, baking soda, brown sugar, and herbs. Stir the egg mixture into the buckwheat sponge along with the melted butter until well blended.

Heat a griddle or heavy skillet over medium heat, and lightly grease it with vegetable oil.

Drop the batter into the hot pan by small tea-spoonfuls. Brown on one side, turn and brown on the other.

Serve immediately topped with sour cream, caviar, smoked salmon, and chopped chive blossoms or chives.

....

Do Ahead: Make the sponge. Stir together the salt, baking soda, brown sugar, and herbs, and cover. Chop chives. This recipe is best done in this manner and finished in the morning. The batter can be prepared entirely the night before.

In the Morning (about 15 minutes): Beat the eggs into the dry ingredients, and stir into the sponge. Cook and garnish the blinis as directed.

....

Corn Pancakes with Smoked Salmon and Dill-Shallot Sauce

These elegantly sauced golden corn cakes are perfect for that breakfast in bed when you want to impress someone special but not have to work too hard.

4 servings

For the Pancakes

1 CUP BOILING WATER

1 CUP CORNMEAL

4 TABLESPOONS BUTTER, CUT INTO PIECES

1 CUP UNBLEACHED WHITE FLOUR

1½ TEASPOONS BAKING POWDER

1 TEASPOON SALT

3 TABLESPOONS SUGAR

3 EGGS

1 CUP MILK

1 OR 2 GREEN ONIONS, SLICED THIN

1 CUP CORN KERNELS (OPTIONAL)

For the Sauce

½ CUP SOUR CREAM

2 TABLESPOONS CHOPPED FRESH DILL

2 TABLESPOONS FINELY CHOPPED SHALLOTS OR RED ONION

DASH OF DRY VERMOUTH OR DRY WHITE WINE (OPTIONAL)

(continued)

To Finish the Dish

Vegetable oil

¼ pound smoked salmon

Sliced green onions and/or dill for garnish

To Make the Pancakes

In a large bowl, pour the boiling water over the cornmeal. Stir in the butter until melted, and set the cornmeal aside to cool for about 10 minutes.

Meanwhile, stir together the flour, baking powder, salt, and sugar in a medium-size bowl. In another bowl, beat the eggs with the milk until well blended, and stir in the green onions and corn.

To Make the Sauce

Stir together the sour cream, dill, shallots, and vermouth. Refrigerate it until ready to use.

When the cornmeal is cool, stir in the egg mixture until smooth. Add the dry ingredients, half at a time, and stir just until blended. Do not overmix.

To Finish the Dish

Heat a griddle or heavy skillet over medium heat, and lightly grease it with vegetable oil. Preheat the oven to 250 degrees.

Drop the batter onto the hot pan by heaping tablespoonfuls. When the pancakes are bubbly on top and nicely browned on the bottom, flip them. As they cook through, transfer them to a baking sheet and keep them warm in the oven while you cook the rest of the batter.

Serve on plates topped with slices of smoked salmon and a generous dollop of the sauce. Garnish with green onions, dill, or both.

....

Do Ahead: The batter can be prepared entirely the night before. Or stir together the dry ingredients and store, covered, at room temperature. Beat the eggs with the milk, green onions, and corn, and refrigerate, covered. Make and refrigerate the sauce.

In the Morning (about 20 minutes): Pour the boiling water over the cornmeal, stir in the butter, and let it cool for about 10 minutes. Finish the batter and cook the pancakes as directed.

....

CRISPY POTATO PANCAKES (LATKES)

We ate these potato pancakes for breakfast and dinner during Chanukah when I was growing up. Like matzo balls, they are so popular with my children that they are no longer just holiday fare. I usually double the recipe because it seems I never have enough.

The key to really crisp pancakes is to thoroughly drain the grated potatoes before mixing in the other ingredients. They are a natural with fresh cooked apples and sour cream, but we also like them with roasted meats and gravy, and with eggs over easy and toast. This recipe was inspired by one in a book my mother gave me when I first took interest in cooking, *The Jewish Home Beautiful* by the National Women's League of the United Synagogue of America (New York, 1949).

4 servings

4 BAKING POTATOES

1½ TEASPOONS SALT

1 MEDIUM ONION

2 EGGS, BEATEN

½ TEASPOON FRESHLY GROUND PEPPER

3 TABLESPOONS UNBLEACHED WHITE FLOUR

1 TEASPOON BAKING POWDER

VEGETABLE OIL

Peel the potatoes and grate them very fine. Put them in a colander and toss with salt. Set the colander over the sink for 15 minutes, pressing the potatoes occasionally to squeeze out the water.

Grate the onion finely and put it in a large bowl. Stir in the eggs, pepper, flour, and baking powder until smooth. Add the drained potatoes and mix thoroughly.

Preheat the oven to 300 degrees.

Heat 2 tablespoons of oil in a heavy skillet over medium heat. Drop the batter into the hot pan by heaping tablespoonfuls, and flatten slightly with a spatula. Brown the pancakes on one side, flip, and brown on the other side. Keep them warm in the oven while you cook the rest of the batter. Serve hot.

. . . .

DO AHEAD: If you drain the potatoes very well, you can make the batter the night before and refrigerate, tightly covered. Don't worry about any graying on the surface.

IN THE MORNING (ABOUT 15 MINUTES): Cook the pancakes as directed.

. . . .

Basic Waffles with Variations

Saturday morning legends are built on great waffles around my town. It seems that the universal key to success is to infuse plenty of fat into the batter to keep it from sticking, which we all know can be a disaster. I use the old-fashioned kind of waffle iron that you put directly over the burner of your gas stove. Whatever kind you have, make sure it's very well seasoned.

4 to 6 waffles

1¾ cups unbleached white flour

2 teaspoons baking powder

½ teaspoon salt

2 tablespoons sugar

3 eggs, separated

1½ cups milk

Optional ingredients (see below)

**7 or 8 tablespoons butter, melted and
cooled slightly**

In a bowl, stir together the flour, baking powder, salt, sugar, and any spices or herbs, if making one of the variations below. In another bowl, beat the egg whites until they hold soft peaks. In a third bowl, beat the egg yolks with the milk and any optional liquid ingredients until smooth.

Mix the dry ingredients and the melted butter into the egg yolk mixture just until smooth. Fold in the beaten egg whites and any optional solid ingredients just until blended.

Heat your waffle iron and bake the waffles according to the manufacturer's instructions, browning and crisping them on both sides.

Optional Ingredients

- For a more aromatic waffle, add 1 teaspoon ground cinnamon and/or ¼ teaspoon nutmeg.
- For a savory waffle, add a generous handful of chopped fresh herbs and a tablespoon or two of grated onion. These waffles are great for dinner topped with old-fashioned creamed chicken or beef.
- For onion waffles, stir in 1 cup chopped and sautéed onion, and increase the salt a bit.
- For spicy waffles that are wonderful with eggs and spicy sausages or smoked meats, stir in 2 tablespoons catsup, ½ teaspoon or more cayenne, 1 teaspoon dry thyme, ½ teaspoon fresh pepper, and 2 minced garlic cloves.
- For curried waffles, which are wonderful with roast chicken, add 2 tablespoons curry powder, 2 tablespoons chopped parsley, and 2 tablespoons grated onion.

Do Ahead: Separate the eggs, and beat the yolks with the other liquid ingredients. Refrigerate the whites and the yolk mixture separately, covered. Stir together the dry ingredients, and store at room temperature. This recipe is best done in this manner and finished in the morning.

In the Morning (about 15 minutes): Heat the griddle, melt the butter, beat the egg whites, and mix and bake the batter as directed.

BUTTERMILK-PECAN WAFFLES

For breakfast, serve these light, nutty waffles with maple syrup warmed with a tablespoon or two of good bourbon. For dinner, add a handful of chopped parsley to the batter.

2 large or 3 average waffles

1 CUP UNBLEACHED WHITE FLOUR (OR ½ CUP WHITE AND ½ CUP WHOLE WHEAT OR BUCKWHEAT)

¼ TEASPOON BAKING SODA

¾ TEASPOON BAKING POWDER

1½ TABLESPOONS SUGAR

PINCH OF SALT

2 EGGS, SEPARATED

1 CUP BUTTERMILK

3 TABLESPOONS MELTED BUTTER, SLIGHTLY COOLED, OR VEGETABLE OIL

⅓ CUP TOASTED PECAN PIECES

In a bowl, stir together the flour, baking soda, baking powder, sugar, and salt. In another bowl, beat the egg whites until they hold soft peaks. In a third bowl, beat the egg yolks with the buttermilk and butter.

Mix the dry ingredients into the egg yolk mixture just until smooth. Fold in the beaten egg whites and pecans just until blended.

Heat your waffle iron and bake the waffles according to the manufacturer's instructions, browning and crisping them on both sides.

Do Ahead: Separate the eggs, and beat the yolks with the buttermilk. Refrigerate the whites and the yolk mixture separately, covered. Stir together the dry ingredients, and store at room temperature. This recipe is best done in this manner and finished in the morning.

In the Morning (about 15 minutes): Heat the griddle, melt the butter, beat the egg whites, and mix and bake the batter as directed.

BREAKFAST WAFFLE SANDWICH

I often use a Croque-Monsieur iron to make breakfast sandwiches, a simple, yet exciting new twist to many combinations that are eaten with toast. Because more households have a waffle iron, I experimented one morning and used it instead. The ridges made from the waffle iron were crispy and delicious and scream for all kinds of creative toppings to complement the filling. This recipe is straightforward and homey. But, the sheer simplicity of it conjured up other more elegant and tasty treats that would work (some suggestions follow the recipe). I even imagined taking my waffle iron camping (it isn't electric) and making smokey ham and cheese breakfast sandwiches over a campfire.

2 servings

2 TEASPOONS UNSALTED BUTTER

¼ CUP CHOPPED WHITE ONION

2 LARGE EGGS

SALT AND FRESHLY GROUND PEPPER

2 OUNCES CHEDDAR OR JACK CHEESE, CUT INTO SMALL, THIN SLICES

4 STANDARD SLICES WHOLE WHEAT OR WHITE BREAD

In a small sauté pan over medium heat, melt 1 teaspoon of the butter. Cook the onions in the butter until soft. Add the eggs and scramble until cooked. Season with salt and pepper.

Heat the waffle iron. Use the remaining teaspoon butter to lightly oil both sides of two sections of the iron. Place 2 pieces of bread on each of the buttered sections. Scoop half the egg mixture onto each piece of bread. Top with the cheese and the remaining slices of bread and close the iron. Brown on each side.

VARIATIONS

- Jelly and Cheddar cheese: top with a dollop of yogurt or sour cream.
- Ham and Swiss cheese: serve with a dipping sauce of mango chutney.
- Fresh raspberries and goat cheese with fresh mint: sprinkle with confectioners' sugar or honey.
- Slices of tomato, mozzarella, and prosciutto: top with 1 tablespoon basil pesto.
- Roasted peppers, eggs, and Asiago cheese: serve with a sprinkling of chopped green onions.

Whole Wheat Sage Waffles with Shiitake Mushroom Gravy

This warming, nurturing dish is a perfect breakfast offering for someone who complains of being cold from the beginning of winter till springtime. If you eat meat, links of good pork sausage are a fine accompaniment. For a richer waffle, replace the ¾ cup milk with ½ cup milk and ¼ cup sour cream.

2 large or 3 average waffles

½ cup whole wheat flour

½ cup unbleached white flour

1 tablespoon wheat germ or unprocessed bran flakes

1 teaspoon baking powder

¼ teaspoon baking soda

½ teaspoon salt

¼ teaspoon freshly ground pepper

2 tablespoons chopped fresh sage leaves

2 eggs, separated

¾ cup milk

4 tablespoons unsalted butter, melted and slightly cooled, or vegetable oil

Shiitake Mushroom Gravy (recipe follows)

In a bowl, stir together the flours, wheat germ, baking powder, baking soda, salt, pepper, and sage. In another bowl, beat the egg whites until they hold soft peaks. In a third bowl, beat the egg yolks with the milk and butter.

Mix the dry ingredients into the egg yolk mixture just until smooth. Fold in the beaten egg whites just until blended.

Heat your waffle iron and bake the waffles according to the manufacturer's instructions, browning and crisping them on both sides.

Serve each waffle topped with about ½ cup Shiitake Mushroom Gravy.

Shiitake Mushroom Gravy

1 tablespoon vegetable oil

1 medium yellow onion, chopped fine

1½ cups thinly sliced fresh shiitake mushrooms

1 teaspoon sweet paprika

Pinch of nutmeg (optional)

3 tablespoons Madeira or other sweet cooking sherry

4 tablespoons unsalted butter

3 tablespoons unbleached white flour

2 cups milk

2 tablespoons chopped fresh parsley

Salt and freshly ground pepper

(continued)

Heat a skillet over medium heat and add the oil. When it's hot, sauté the onion and mushrooms until soft, about 5 minutes, stirring occasionally.

Turn the heat to high, stir in the paprika, nutmeg, and Madeira, and cook a minute longer. Take the pan off the heat and set it aside.

Melt the butter in a saucepan over medium heat. Whisk in the flour and cook, stirring constantly, for about 3 minutes. Slowly add the milk, whisking constantly until the sauce thickens, 3 to 5 minutes.

Stir in the mushroom mixture and any pan juices, the parsley, and salt and pepper to taste. Add more nutmeg if you like.

. . . .

DO AHEAD: Separate the eggs, and beat the yolks with the milk. Refrigerate the whites and the yolk mixture separately, covered. Stir together the dry ingredients, and store at room temperature. Make and refrigerate the gravy. This recipe is best done in this manner and finished in the morning.

IN THE MORNING (ABOUT 15 MINUTES): Heat the griddle, melt the butter, beat the egg whites, and mix and bake the batter as directed. Reheat the gravy.

. . . .

DAY AFTER THANKSGIVING SWEET POTATO WAFFLES WITH TURKEY, PEAS, AND CARROTS

Imagine presenting this breakfast to someone who is snuggled up under a quilt in front of the television, watching a post-Thanksgiving football game or Saturday morning cartoons! In lieu of peas and carrots, you can use leftover vegetables from the holiday feast in the sauce. Or forget the sauce and top the waffles with leftover gravy and bits of turkey. For sweet waffles, omit the pepper and herbs from the batter and add 2 tablespoons of brown sugar; serve them for breakfast topped with maple syrup and toasted walnuts or pecans.

4 servings

FOR THE SAUCE

4 TABLESPOONS BUTTER

3 TABLESPOONS UNBLEACHED WHITE FLOUR

3 CUPS TURKEY OR CHICKEN STOCK

SALT AND FRESHLY GROUND PEPPER

FOR THE WAFFLES

3 EGGS, SEPARATED

1½ CUPS MASHED COOKED YAMS

1 CUP MILK

½ CUP (1 STICK) BUTTER, MELTED AND SLIGHTLY COOLED

1½ cups unbleached white flour

2 teaspoons baking powder

1 teaspoon salt

½ teaspoon freshly ground pepper

1½ teaspoons dried sage leaves

2 tablespoons chopped fresh parsley

To Finish the Dish

1½ cups chopped cooked turkey

1½ cups cooked peas and carrots or other leftover vegetables

Turkey or chicken stock

Chopped parsley for garnish

To Make the Sauce

Melt the butter in a saucepan over medium heat. Add the flour and cook, stirring constantly, for about 3 minutes. Gradually add the stock, stirring until it thickens. Season with salt and pepper. Keep the sauce warm over very low heat while you make the waffles.

To make the waffles, beat the egg yolks with the yams, milk, and melted butter until smooth. In another bowl, stir together the flour, baking powder, salt, pepper, sage, and parsley. In a third bowl, beat the egg whites until they hold soft peaks.

Mix the dry ingredients into the egg yolk mixture just until smooth. Fold in the beaten egg whites just until blended.

Heat your waffle iron and bake the waffles according to the manufacturer's instructions, browning and crisping them on both sides.

While the waffles are baking, warm the turkey and vegetables in a little stock on the stove or, similarly, in the microwave.

To serve, put the waffles on plates, mound turkey and vegetables on top, and pour sauce over all. Garnish with parsley and serve. Leftovers will keep in the refrigerator for two days.

....

Do Ahead: Separate the eggs, and beat the yolks with the milk and yams. Refrigerate the whites and the yolk mixture separately, covered. Stir together the dry ingredients, and store at room temperature. Make and refrigerate the sauce. This recipe is best done in this manner and finished in the morning.

In the Morning (20 to 30 minutes): Heat the griddle, melt the butter, beat the egg whites, and mix and bake the batter as directed. Reheat the gravy and the turkey and vegetables, and assemble the dish.

....

Baked Goods

It was a cool summer morning. The aroma of something baking in the oven came drifting into the bedroom, stirring me from sleep. It was a day to sleep in, and it never crossed my mind that a conspiracy was in the making to surprise me with breakfast in bed.

My son and my love had secretly assembled the ingredients to make Spicy Buttermilk-Corn-Basil Biscuits (page 87), a favorite of mine. When I tried to get up and give a hand, they whisked me to the backyard. They had created an outside bed for me: a cushy lawn chair covered with a cotton sheet and blanket and my favorite pillow. A cup of English breakfast tea fixed perfectly to my liking with a hint of honey and lots of milk was on the table next to the book I was reading. A small antique bowl with three freshly cut gardenia blossoms filled the air with my favorite fragrance. My backyard is like a giant aviary, and the birds seemed to be singing to me, softly, sweetly.

Had I died and gone to heaven? Was it Mother's Day? My birthday?

Within about half an hour, a tray of food was placed before me. They propped up the pillows, straightened the blanket, smoothed a flowered napkin on my lap, and presented me with a morning feast. The biscuits were accompanied by scrambled eggs topped with sweet caramelized onions, wedges of fresh melon, and a glass of fruity gewürztraminer. I ate slowly. All my senses felt fully alive. The exquisite food, the smell of the morning sun on the still-damp patio, the singing of the birds—heaven on earth.

Now and forever, the smell of fresh-baked bread, biscuits, muffins, or coffee cake in the morning reminds me of that magic moment. Thank you, guys.

CINNAMON–BROWN SUGAR DROP BISCUITS

With the cinnamon and brown sugar melted within, these fill the kitchen with irresistible aromas. They often get eaten straight off the baking sheet, warm, moist, and flavorful.

About 20 biscuits

FOR THE DOUGH

1½ CUPS UNBLEACHED WHITE FLOUR

½ CUP WHOLE WHEAT FLOUR

2 TEASPOONS BAKING POWDER

1 TEASPOON BAKING SODA

½ TEASPOON SALT

½ CUP (1 STICK) BUTTER, CHILLED AND CUT
    INTO PIECES

ABOUT ¾ CUP MILK OR APPLE JUICE

FOR THE FILLING

1 TABLESPOON CINNAMON

2 TABLESPOONS UNBLEACHED WHITE FLOUR

2 TABLESPOONS BUTTER, SOFTENED

½ CUP PACKED BROWN SUGAR

Preheat the oven to 400 degrees. Lightly oil one large or two average baking sheets.

TO MAKE THE BATTER

Stir together the flours, baking powder, baking soda, and salt in a medium-size bowl. With a pastry blender or your hands, cut in the butter until the mixture is grainy. Stir in enough milk to form a dough, just moist enough to plop from a spoon.

TO MAKE THE FILLING

Stir together the cinnamon, flour, butter, and brown sugar in a small bowl until well mixed.

To form each biscuit, drop a generous teaspoon of dough onto the prepared sheet. Crumble about ½ teaspoon of the topping into the center. Top with another teaspoon of dough, followed by a final ½ teaspoon of topping mix. Continue dropping biscuits, about 2 inches apart. Bake until flaky and lightly browned, about 10 minutes.

Freeze any unbaked biscuits on a tray or baking sheet and then transfer them to an airtight container. When ready to bake, place them on baking sheets, let stand at room temperature for 10 minutes, and bake as directed.

. . . .

DO AHEAD: Make the dough, mix the filling, and refrigerate separately, tightly covered, overnight.

IN THE MORNING (ABOUT 20 MINUTES): Preheat the oven, and assemble and bake the biscuits.

. . . .

SOUR CREAM, ORANGE, AND LAVENDER BISCUITS

I like to serve these delicate biscuits with honey butter and wedges of just-picked oranges from my neighbor's prolific orange tree. Use fresh blossoms if you're lucky enough to have access to a lavender bush, or look for dried blossoms at a natural foods or spice store. Rosemary may be substituted.

12 to 14 biscuits

2 CUPS UNBLEACHED WHITE FLOUR

½ TEASPOON SALT

1 TABLESPOON BAKING POWDER

1 TABLESPOON SUGAR

4 OR MORE TABLESPOONS FINELY GRATED ORANGE ZEST

2 TABLESPOONS CHOPPED LAVENDER BLOSSOMS OR 1 TABLESPOON CHOPPED FRESH ROSEMARY

ABOUT 1¼ CUPS SOUR CREAM

Preheat the oven to 400 degrees. Lightly oil one large or two average baking sheets.

Stir together the flour, salt, baking powder, sugar, orange zest, and lavender in a large bowl. Gradually stir in enough sour cream to form a sticky dough.

Turn the dough onto a floured board. Knead by gently folding the dough in half a dozen times or so until it no longer sticks to the board. Roll or press it into a ½-inch thickness.

Use a cookie cutter or sharp knife to cut the dough into 2-inch rounds. Place them on the prepared sheet, and bake them until lightly browned, about 12 minutes.

Freeze any unbaked biscuits on a tray or baking sheet and then transfer them to an airtight container. When ready to bake, place them on baking sheets, let stand at room temperature for 10 minutes, and bake as directed.

. . . .

DO AHEAD: Mix the dough, cut out the biscuits, and refrigerate them on the baking sheets, covered with a cotton dish towel.

IN THE MORNING (15 TO 20 MINUTES): Preheat the oven and bake as directed.

. . . .

WHOLE WHEAT SCONES WITH RAISINS OR DRIED CRANBERRIES

This is an adaptation of a recipe created by Bob Cool, my former husband and partner, at our first restaurant, Late for the Train. The dough can be made in large batches, cut out, and frozen for weeks.

24 scones

1 CUP (2 STICKS) UNSALTED BUTTER

5 CUPS UNBLEACHED WHITE FLOUR

1½ CUPS WHOLE WHEAT FLOUR

¾ TEASPOON SALT

2½ TEASPOONS BAKING POWDER

¾ TEASPOON BAKING SODA

¾ CUP RAISINS OR DRIED CRANBERRIES

¼ CUP SUGAR

3 EGGS

2 CUPS BUTTERMILK

Preheat the oven to 350 degrees. Lightly oil a baking sheet.

Melt the butter in a saucepan over medium heat, and set it aside.

Stir together the flours, salt, baking powder, baking soda, and raisins in a medium bowl.

In a large bowl, beat the sugar with the eggs and buttermilk.

Add about two-thirds of the dry ingredients to the wet ingredients, and mix until just blended (I use my hands). Add the melted butter and the remaining dry ingredients, and mix lightly.

Turn the dough onto a floured surface, and knead by flattening and folding it about ten times, until it no longer sticks.

Let the dough rest for about 5 minutes. Roll it out to a thickness of about 1½ inches. Cut it into 2-inch rounds with a cookie cutter or glass. Place as many as will be eaten in the morning on the baking sheet about 1 inch apart. Bake until lightly browned, 20 to 25 minutes.

Freeze the remaining rounds in an airtight container. When ready to bake, place them on baking sheets, let stand at room temperature for 10 minutes, and bake as directed.

. . . .

DO AHEAD: Mix and cut out the dough, and put the scones on the baking sheet. Refrigerate them, covered with a kitchen towel, overnight. Or freeze the dough, and transfer the frozen dough to a freezer bag or other airtight container. It will keep for 2 days in the refrigerator and for several weeks in the freezer.

IN THE MORNING: Preheat the oven, and bake the scones. They will take about 5 minutes longer because the dough is cold.

. . . .

Spicy Buttermilk-Corn-Basil Biscuits

These biscuits are a flavorful accompaniment to Steamed Eggs with Quick Ranchero Sauce (page 34) or eggs scrambled with green onions or chives. Adjust the amount of chile peppers depending on how hot they are.

About 12 biscuits

2 CUPS UNBLEACHED WHITE FLOUR

1 CUP YELLOW CORNMEAL

3 TABLESPOONS BAKING POWDER

½ TEASPOON SALT

ABOUT 2 TEASPOONS CRUMBLED DRIED CHILE PEPPERS OR RED PEPPER FLAKES

2 TABLESPOONS LIGHT BROWN SUGAR

½ CUP (1 STICK) BUTTER, CHILLED AND CUT INTO PIECES

1½ CUPS BUTTERMILK

1 CUP FINELY CHOPPED FRESH BASIL

KERNELS FROM 1 MEDIUM EAR SWEET CORN (ABOUT 1 CUP), COOKED

1 CUP GRATED CHEDDAR CHEESE

Preheat the oven to 400 degrees. Lightly oil one large or two average baking sheets.

Stir together the flour, cornmeal, baking powder, salt, chiles, and sugar in a large bowl. Cut in the butter with a pastry blender until the mixture is grainy. (Or combine the dry ingredients in a food processor and pulse to blend in the butter.) Add the buttermilk, basil, and corn, and stir just until blended.

Turn the dough onto a floured surface, and knead by flattening and folding it about ten times, until it no longer sticks. Roll it out to a thickness of about 1½ inches, and sprinkle it with the cheese. Cut it into 2-inch rounds with a cookie cutter or glass, and place them on the baking sheet about 1 inch apart. Refrigerate for 30 minutes to chill the butter in the dough. Bake for about 15 minutes, until golden brown.

Freeze any unbaked biscuits in an airtight container. When ready to bake, place them on baking sheets, let stand at room temperature for 10 minutes, and bake as directed.

....

DO AHEAD: Cook the corn and combine it with the buttermilk. Stir together the dry ingredients, chiles, and basil, and cut in the butter. Refrigerate all, covered.

IN THE MORNING (ABOUT 30 MINUTES): Preheat the oven. Combine the wet and dry ingredients. Knead, roll out, and cut the dough. Bake the biscuits.

....

HERB–LEMON ZEST POPOVERS

In James Beard's *American Cookery* (Boston: Little Brown, 1972), I learned a way to cook popovers that's perfect for breakfast in bed. Instead of having to pour the batter into a sizzling hot pan, you can start it in a cold oven.

I like to serve these with scrambled eggs with chives and strawberries with crème fraîche (page 7). Break a warm popover in half on each plate, fill it with scrambled eggs, surround it with sliced strawberries, and garnish the berries with crème fraîche.

3 EGGS

1 CUP MILK

1 CUP UNBLEACHED WHITE FLOUR

½ TEASPOON SALT

¼ TEASPOON FRESHLY GROUND BLACK PEPPER

2 TEASPOONS GRATED LEMON ZEST

½ TEASPOON CHOPPED FRESH THYME (OPTIONAL)

2 TABLESPOONS BUTTER, MELTED

Separate the eggs, and beat the whites until they hold soft peaks.

In another bowl, beat the yolks with the milk until well blended.

In a third bowl, stir together the flour, salt, pepper, lemon zest, and thyme.

Stir the milk mixture into the dry ingredients just until blended. Stir in the butter. Don't overmix or the popovers will be tough. Fold in the egg whites.

Pour the batter into twelve small or ten medium-sized muffin tins, filling them two-thirds full.

Put the pan in a cold oven, and turn the heat to 425 degrees. Bake for about 30 minutes, until the popovers are puffed and browned. Remove them from the oven and run a small, sharp knife around each cup to loosen the popovers from the pan.

....

DO AHEAD: Separate the eggs. Whisk the yolks with the milk in one bowl, put the whites in another bowl, and refrigerate, covered. Combine the flour, salt, pepper, lemon zest, and thyme, and store, covered, at room temperature.

IN THE MORNING (30 TO 40 MINUTES): Preheat the oven. Beat the egg whites, melt the butter, and assemble and bake the batter as directed.

....

A SELECTION OF SWEET AND SAVORY MUFFINS

SWEET MUFFINS WITH VARIATIONS

Use one or more of the variations given, or let your imagination and common cooking sense guide you to new heights of muffin delights. When we tested these at Flea St., we added a cup of ripe banana, pecans, and a generous teaspoon of cinnamon to the batter.

9 to 12 muffins

½ CUP UNSALTED BUTTER, SOFTENED

1 CUP WHITE OR FIRMLY PACKED LIGHT BROWN SUGAR

2 LARGE EGGS, BEATEN

½ CUP SOUR CREAM, MILK, OR FRUIT JUICE

2 TEASPOONS VANILLA EXTRACT

1⅔ CUPS UNBLEACHED WHITE FLOUR OR 1 CUP WHITE FLOUR AND ⅔ CUP WHOLE WHEAT FLOUR

2 TEASPOONS BAKING POWDER

OPTIONAL INGREDIENTS (SEE VARIATIONS)

PINCH OF SALT

Preheat the oven to 375 degrees. Grease a muffin tin or line it with paper muffin cups; you will need nine for the basic batter and twelve if you add fruit.

Beat the butter with the sugar in a large bowl until light and fluffy. Beat in the eggs, sour cream, and vanilla.

In another bowl, stir together the flour, baking powder, any spices, and salt.

Add the dry ingredients to the wet, and stir just until blended. Fold in any fruit (see Variations below). Don't overmix or the muffins will be tough.

Spoon the batter into the prepared tin, filling the cups about two-thirds full. Bake for about 20 minutes, until lightly browned and springy to the touch. Let the muffins cool in the pan for 5 minutes before transferring them to a cooling rack. Serve warm. Store leftover muffins in an airtight container.

VARIATIONS

- Fold 1 cup of fresh or dry fruit bits into the batter just before baking.
- Add a cup of pureed fruit such as bananas, applesauce, or mashed strawberries to the batter just before baking.
- Make a crumb topping by crumbling together ½ cup cold butter, ⅓ cup brown sugar, ¼ cup rolled oats, and if you like, ¼ cup chopped nuts. Sprinkle it on the muffins just before baking.
- Replace 2 tablespoons of the flour with wheat germ.

- Drop a tablespoon of jam in the center of each muffin before baking.
- Grate lots of lemon, lime, or orange zest into the batter.
- Create upside-down fruit muffins by placing a teaspoon of butter, a tablespoon of brown sugar, and a thin layer of chopped fresh fruit such as bananas in the muffin cup before adding the batter.

·······································

Do Ahead: Cream the butter with the sugar, and let it sit out, covered, overnight. Beat the eggs with the sour cream and vanilla, and refrigerate. Stir together the dry ingredients and cover. Prepare any fruit, crumb topping, etc., if making a Variation.

In the Morning (about 30 minutes): Preheat the oven. Beat the liquids into the butter mixture. Add the dry ingredients, and finish the muffins as directed.

·······································

SAVORY MUFFINS WITH VARIATIONS

Bits of salty meat, flavorful vegetables, pungent cheese, herbs and spices, or even roasted garlic turn a muffin into a savory breakfast experience. If you like, substitute whole wheat flour or wheat bran for 1 cup of the unbleached white flour.

About 12 muffins

2 CUPS UNBLEACHED WHITE FLOUR

2 TEASPOONS BAKING POWDER

2 TABLESPOONS SUGAR

½ TEASPOON SALT

½ TEASPOON BLACK OR RED PEPPER (OPTIONAL)

2 LARGE EGGS

1 CUP MILK, SOUR CREAM, YOGURT, OR BUTTERMILK

⅓ CUP VEGETABLE, OLIVE, AVOCADO, OR CANOLA OIL

1 CUP OR LESS OPTIONAL INGREDIENTS (SEE VARIATIONS BELOW)

Preheat the oven to 375 degrees. Generously butter a muffin tin. The basic recipe yields about a dozen muffins; depending on the optional ingredients, you may get a few more.

Stir together the flour, baking powder, sugar, salt, and pepper in a large bowl.

In another bowl, beat the eggs, milk, and oil.

Pour the wet ingredients into the dry, and stir just until combined; don't overmix or the muffins will be tough. Fold in any optional ingredients.

Spoon the batter into the prepared tin, filling the cups about two-thirds full. Bake for about 20 minutes, until the muffins are lightly browned and springy to the touch. Let them cool in the pan for 5 minutes before transferring to a cooling rack. Serve warm. Store leftover muffins in an airtight container.

VARIATIONS

Use any combination of additional ingredients you like, up to 1 cup total.

- Grated cheese such as Swiss, Emmenthaler, flavored Brie, Camembert, sharp Cheddar, any kind of blue cheese or smoked cheese
- Chopped cooked ham, bacon, prosciutto, sausage, or smoked chicken
- Flaked smoked salmon or whitefish
- Chopped fresh herbs or garlic
- Cooked or raw red, white, yellow, or green onions
- Mashed roasted garlic
- Capers or sliced olives

. . . .

DO AHEAD: Stir together and cover the dry ingredients. Beat together and refrigerate the wet ingredients, covered. Chop or otherwise prepare any optional ingredients, and refrigerate if necessary.

IN THE MORNING (ABOUT 30 MINUTES): Preheat the oven. Stir the wet ingredients into the dry, fold in any optional ingredients, and bake the muffins as directed.

. . . .

PEAR SPICE CAKE WITH GORGONZOLA–CREAM CHEESE ICING

On cold fall mornings, I sometimes wake up craving something sweet and moist, like this cake. My neighbors Cal and Helen got a wedge of the first one I baked, and were enthralled by the combination of sweet pears and pungent cheese. It's a great use for overripe pears, and it's even better the day after it's baked.

10 to 12 servings

FOR THE BATTER

½ CUP WHITE SUGAR

1 CUP LIGHT BROWN SUGAR

¾ CUP VEGETABLE OIL

4 EGGS

2 TEASPOONS VANILLA EXTRACT

2 CUPS UNBLEACHED WHITE FLOUR

½ CUP OLD-FASHIONED ROLLED OATS

2 TEASPOONS BAKING POWDER

1 TEASPOON BAKING SODA

2 ROUNDED TEASPOONS GROUND CINNAMON

1 TEASPOON GROUND NUTMEG

½ TEASPOON GROUND CLOVES

3 CUPS GRATED PEELED RIPE PEARS
   (3 MEDIUM PEARS)

1 CUP CHOPPED WALNUTS

(continued)

FOR THE ICING

10 OUNCES CREAM CHEESE, SOFTENED

2 TO 3 OUNCES GORGONZOLA CHEESE,
SOFTENED

1½ CUPS GRATED PEELED RIPE PEARS,
(1½ MEDIUM PEARS)

MILK

Preheat the oven to 350 degrees. Generously butter a 10-inch springform or Bundt pan.

TO MAKE THE BATTER

Beat together the sugars, oil, eggs, and vanilla until well blended. In another bowl, stir together the flour, oats, baking powder, baking soda, and spices. Add half the flour mixture to the wet ingredients, and beat just until blended. Mix in the remaining flour mixture, and fold in the pears and walnuts. Do not overbeat.

Pour the batter into the prepared pan, and bake for 45 minutes to 1 hour, until a toothpick inserted into the center of the cake comes out clean. Cool on a rack for 30 minutes before removing from the pan.

TO MAKE THE ICING

While the cake is cooling, beat the cream cheese, cheese, and pears together with an electric mixer or by hand. Add milk a teaspoon at a time until the icing is smooth and spreadable.

Remove the cooled cake from the pan, spread it with icing or serve it on the side. Refrigerate or freeze leftovers.

....

DO AHEAD: The cake is even better the second day. Store it at room temperature overnight, and in the refrigerator thereafter.

IN THE MORNING (ABOUT 5 MINUTES): Cut and serve the cake.

....

CINNAMON-PECAN CRUMB CAKE WITH WARM APPLESAUCE

My friend Beth Hensperger created this moist, scrumptious crumb cake. She swears that when it comes out of her oven, friends and neighbors suddenly appear.

10 to 12 servings

BOTTOM TO TOP: PEAR SPICE CAKE WITH GORGONZOLA–CREAM CHEESE ICING (PAGE 93),
CINNAMON–PECAN CRUMB CAKE WITH WARM APPLESAUCE

For the Topping

2 CUPS UNBLEACHED WHITE FLOUR

1 CUP LIGHT BROWN SUGAR

1½ TABLESPOONS GROUND CINNAMON

15 TABLESPOONS (1 CUP MINUS 1 TABLE-
SPOON) UNSALTED BUTTER, CHILLED

¾ CUP CHOPPED PECANS

For the Batter

6 TABLESPOONS UNSALTED BUTTER, SOFTENED

¾ CUP BROWN SUGAR

3 EGGS, BEATEN

1 TABLESPOON VANILLA EXTRACT

2 CUPS UNBLEACHED WHITE FLOUR

1 TEASPOON BAKING POWDER

1 TEASPOON BAKING SODA

½ TEASPOON SALT

1 CUP SOUR CREAM OR BUTTERMILK

2 CUPS APPLESAUCE

To Make the Topping

Stir together the flour, sugar, and cinnamon. Cut the butter into small pieces, and cut it into the flour mixture with a pastry blender or knife until crumb-like. (Or mix the dry ingredients in a food processor; pulse in the butter.) Stir in the pecans. Refrigerate.

Preheat the oven to 350 degrees. Generously butter a 10-inch springform pan.

To Make the Batter

Cream the butter and sugar with an electric mixer until fluffy and light. Beat in the eggs one at a time, and then the vanilla.

In another bowl, stir together the flour, baking powder, soda, and salt. Beat half of it into the egg mixture just until blended. Add the rest of the dry ingredients and the sour cream, and beat just until smooth. Do not overmix.

Spread half the batter in the prepared pan, and sprinkle it with one-third of the topping mixture. Spread on the remaining batter, and sprinkle on the rest of the topping.

Bake for about 45 minutes, until a toothpick inserted into the center of the cake comes out relatively dry. Do not overbake or the cake will be dry.

Run a knife around the inside of the pan to loosen the cake. Let it cool on a rack for 30 minutes before removing the sides of the pan.

Just before serving, heat the applesauce until very warm. Spoon generous dollops of it over each piece of cake.

....

DO AHEAD: Make and refrigerate the topping. Grease the pan, cream the butter and sugar, mix together the dry ingredients, and store, covered, at room temperature.

IN THE MORNING (ABOUT 1 HOUR): Preheat the oven. Beat the eggs and vanilla into the butter-sugar mixture. Beat in the dry ingredients and sour cream and assemble and bake the cake as directed.

....

HOMINY–RED ONION BREAD WITH CHIPOTLE BUTTER

This spicy, big-flavored bread was such a big hit with the staff at Flea St. when my pastry chef, Christine Gutierrez, tested it that it's sure to end up on the restaurant's brunch menu.

8 to 10 servings

FOR THE BREAD

1 CUP HOMINY GRITS

2 CUPS HOT MILK

1 CUP UNBLEACHED WHITE FLOUR

1 TABLESPOON BAKING POWDER

1 TEASPOON SALT

½ CUP MAPLE SYRUP

6 TABLESPOONS VEGETABLE OIL

2 EGGS, BEATEN

¾ CUP GRATED RED ONION

FOR THE CHIPOTLE BUTTER

4 TABLESPOONS UNSALTED BUTTER, SOFTENED

2 GENEROUS TEASPOONS CHOPPED CANNED CHIPOTLE CHILES

¼ CUP FINELY CHOPPED CHIVES

Put the grits in a medium-size bowl, pour on the hot milk, and let it sit until cool, about 15 minutes.

Preheat the oven to 375 degrees. Generously butter an 8-inch square baking pan.

In a large bowl, stir together the flour, baking powder, and salt, and set aside.

Whisk the maple syrup, oil, eggs, and onion into the cooled grits. Gradually add the dry ingredients, stirring just until combined.

Spread the batter into the prepared pan, and bake it for about 30 minutes, until the top is lightly browned and a toothpick inserted in the center comes out clean. Let it cool in the pan for 15 minutes.

While the bread is cooling, stir together the softened butter, chipotle chiles, and chives.

To serve, cut the bread into squares and spread it with the chipotle butter.

....

DO AHEAD: Pour the milk over the grits; in another bowl, whisk together the maple syrup, oil, eggs, and onion. Refrigerate, covered, overnight. Stir together the dry ingredients, make the chipotle butter, and store, covered, at room temperature overnight. Grease and cover the baking pan.

IN THE MORNING (ABOUT 45 MINUTES): Preheat the oven. Combine the grits and the maple syrup mixture, adding about ¼ cup more milk. Finish the batter and bake the bread as directed.

....

BACON, CHEDDAR, AND PARSLEY SODA BREAD

Cheddar cheese and bacon add an American dinerlike flavor to this variation on traditional Irish soda bread.

8 to 10 servings

1 CUP WHOLE WHEAT PASTRY FLOUR

1 CUP UNBLEACHED WHITE FLOUR

1½ TEASPOONS BAKING POWDER

1 TEASPOON BAKING SODA

½ TEASPOON SALT

2 TABLESPOONS UNSALTED BUTTER, CHILLED

¾ CUP BUTTERMILK OR PLAIN YOGURT

1 EGG, BEATEN

1 TABLESPOON HONEY

1 CUP GRATED CHEDDAR CHEESE

¾ CUP CRUMBLED FRIED BACON (ABOUT 5 SLICES)

¾ CUP THINLY SLICED GREEN ONIONS

Preheat the oven to 375 degrees. Generously grease a baking sheet or line it with parchment paper.

In a large bowl, stir together the flours, baking powder, baking soda, and salt. Or whirl them in a food processor. Cut the butter in with a pastry blender or pulse it with the food processor to form a coarse, cornmeal-like mixture. Remove to a bowl.

In a medium bowl, whisk together the buttermilk, egg, and honey. Add the liquid to the dry ingredients, one-third at a time, stirring just until blended. Fold in the cheese, bacon, and onions. The dough will be moist.

Turn the dough out onto a floured surface, and gently knead it for 3 or 4 minutes, until it's smooth and no longer sticky. Form it into one large loaf or four small ones, and place it on the baking sheet.

Bake it until it's nicely browned, and a toothpick inserted in the center comes out clean, about 35 minutes for small loaves and 45 minutes for a large one. Let it cool on a rack for 10 minutes before slicing.

....

DO AHEAD: Mix the dry ingredients together and cut in the butter. Whisk together the wet ingredients. Grate the cheese, fry and crumble the bacon, and slice the green onions. Refrigerate all, covered.

IN THE MORNING (ABOUT 1 HOUR): Preheat the oven, mix the dough, and bake the bread as directed.

....

SAGE AND ONION PITA BREAD

This recipe was inspired by one in *Flatbreads* by Jeffrey Alford and Naomi Duguid (New York: William Morrow, 1995). Flat breads are "baked" on a very hot griddle or skillet. This is a perfect dough to take along in your cooler on a camping trip. Cook it on that well-seasoned camping skillet, crawl back into your sleeping bag, and enjoy!

About 2 dozen small pita breads

2 TEASPOONS ACTIVE DRY YEAST

1¾ CUPS LUKEWARM WATER

4 CUPS UNBLEACHED WHITE FLOUR

2 CUPS WHOLE WHEAT FLOUR

1 TABLESPOON SALT

⅓ CUP CHOPPED FRESH SAGE

1½ CUPS GRATED RED OR YELLOW ONION AND JUICES

OLIVE OIL

In a large bowl, sprinkle the yeast over the warm water, and set it aside for a few minutes until it's bubbly. Gradually add 3 cups of the white flour, stirring until smooth. Cover and let it rise in a warm spot for about three hours to form a sponge. It will be soft and about double in size.

In a medium bowl, mix the remaining cup of white flour and the whole wheat flour, salt, and sage.

Spread the onions with their juices on top of the sponge. Gradually stir in the whole wheat flour mixture to form a very stiff dough.

Turn the dough onto a floured board and knead for about 5 minutes, until smooth and no longer sticky.

Wipe out the large bowl and lightly coat it with olive oil. Return the dough to the bowl, and turn to coat it with oil on all sides. Cover and let it rise for about 2 hours, until double in size.

Punch down the dough, and store it in an airtight container in the refrigerator.

When ready to use, pinch off a small handful of dough for each pita and form it into a round about 4 inches across and ½ inch thick. Heat a heavy, well-seasoned skillet or griddle over medium-high heat. Working in batches, cook the dough until lightly browned and slightly puffy, about 3 minutes on each side. Serve hot.

. . . .

DO AHEAD: Make the dough, and refrigerate it after the second rising.

IN THE MORNING (ABOUT 15 MINUTES): Heat the pan, and form and cook the pitas as directed.

. . . .

SWEET POTATO HOME FRIES (PAGE 107)

Side Orders

There are times when people are in the mood for eggs or a big hearty breakfast, and other times when a plate of crispy potatoes and onions is just the thing. The side dishes in this chapter will add interest to any breakfast. Piperade or a big spoonful of homemade salsa can transform a plate of eggs and toast. And some of these dishes, like the seafood and corned beef hashes, are meals in themselves.

When I cook breakfast or forage for leftovers, it's usually the potatoes I go for first. Try baking or boiling a few extra when making dinner so that you have a head start on marvelous home fries or hash browns. Substituting sweet potatoes for regular potatoes can add a nice twist. Try drizzling Sweet Potato Home Fries with maple syrup and serving them with a thick slice of grilled ham. Skip the eggs altogether.

Leftover polenta is another godsend in the morning. You can grill or fry it and serve it with tomato sauce, salsa, or maple syrup. Imagine it coming to you on a bed tray next to a bowl of berries, a soft-cooked egg, and a fresh cup of your favorite coffee.

TROPICAL FRUIT SALSA

Salsa can add a burst of flavor and a dash of style to the humblest plate of scrambled eggs. The key to a great salsa is to use the best in-season fruits or vegetables you can find.

Makes about 3 cups

2 GENEROUS CUPS CHOPPED FRESH PINEAPPLE

½ SMALL RED ONION, CHOPPED FINE

¼ CUP CHOPPED CILANTRO

1 TABLESPOON BROWN SUGAR

½ TEASPOON CUMIN

PINCH OF SALT

CHOPPED FRESH OR DRIED HOT CHILE PEPPERS TO TASTE (OPTIONAL)

Stir together all the ingredients in a small bowl. Taste and add more salt if you like. Refrigerate, covered, for at least 15 minutes before serving for flavors to blend.

. . . .

DO AHEAD: The salsa can be made up to 2 days before serving, and refrigerated, covered. It's actually better the next day.

. . . .

CUCUMBER–RED PEPPER SALSA

Leaving a little peel on the cucumber adds color to the salsa. You can substitute 2 tablespoons chopped fresh dill or tarragon for the cilantro.

Makes about 2 cups

1 MEDIUM CUCUMBER, PARTIALLY PEELED AND CHOPPED MEDIUM FINE

½ CUP FINELY CHOPPED RED BELL PEPPER

½ SMALL RED ONION, CHOPPED FINE

1 GARLIC CLOVE, MINCED

¼ CUP CHOPPED CILANTRO OR FRESH BASIL

PINCH OF SALT

CHOPPED FRESH OR DRIED HOT CHILE PEPPERS TO TASTE (OPTIONAL)

Stir together all the ingredients in a small bowl. Taste and add more salt if you like. Refrigerate, covered, for at least 15 minutes before serving for flavors to blend.

. . . .

DO AHEAD: The salsa can be made up to 2 days before serving, and refrigerated, covered.

. . . .

STRAWBERRY MINT SALSA

Use raspberries or blackberries instead of straw-berries if you like.

Makes about 2 cups

1 PINT FRESH STRAWBERRIES
2 TO 3 TABLESPOONS FINELY CHOPPED FRESH
  SPEARMINT
1 GREEN ONION, SLICED THIN
1 TABLESPOON BALSAMIC VINEGAR
PINCH OF SALT
CHOPPED FRESH OR DRIED HOT CHILE PEPPERS
  TO TASTE (OPTIONAL)

Stir together all the ingredients in a small bowl. Taste and add more salt if you like. Refrigerate, covered, for at least 15 minutes before serving for flavors to blend.

....

DO AHEAD: The salsa can be made up to 2 days before serving, and refrigerated, covered.

....

FRESH TOMATO, BASIL, AND CORN SALSA

Makes about 3 cups

1 OR 2 MEDIUM SUN-RIPENED TOMATOES,
  SEEDED AND COARSELY CHOPPED
½ MEDIUM ONION, CHOPPED FINE
½ CUP COOKED CORN KERNELS
½ CUP CHOPPED FRESH BASIL
JUICE OF 1 LIME
PINCH OF SALT
1 TEASPOON EXTRA-VIRGIN OLIVE OIL
  (OPTIONAL)
CHOPPED FRESH OR DRIED HOT CHILE PEPPERS
  TO TASTE (OPTIONAL)

Stir together all the ingredients in a small bowl. Taste and add more salt if you like. Refrigerate, covered, for at least 15 minutes before serving for flavors to blend.

....

DO AHEAD: The salsa can be made up to 2 days before serving, and refrigerated, covered.

....

MANGO SALSA

About 3 cups

2 MEDIUM RIPE MANGOES, PEELED, SEEDED,
  AND DICED
½ CUP CHOPPED CILANTRO
½ SMALL RED ONION, CHOPPED
½ SMALL RED BELL PEPPER, CHOPPED FINE
SPLASH OF LIME JUICE OR RICE WINE VINEGAR
1 TEASPOON CUMIN

Stir together all the ingredients in a medium-size bowl. Taste and add more lime juice if you like. Refrigerate, covered, for at least 15 minutes before serving for flavors to blend.

. . . .

DO AHEAD: The salsa can be made up to 1 day before serving, and refrigerated, covered.

. . . .

GRILLED OR FRIED POLENTA

There are endless ways to serve this nourishing dish—with maple syrup, chopped tomatoes and basil, poached eggs and salsa, fried sausage, peppers and onions, mascarpone, or grated aged cheese. If you don't have time to make the polenta ahead and grill it, serve it soft as you would grits.

6 to 8 servings

5 CUPS WATER, VEGETABLE STOCK, OR
  CHICKEN STOCK
1 CUP CORNMEAL
2 TO 3 TABLESPOONS CHOPPED FRESH
  ROSEMARY, OREGANO, OR THYME
SALT
OLIVE OIL OR BUTTER

Bring the water to a boil in a saucepan. Gradually stir in the cornmeal. Reduce the heat to a simmer and cook, stirring frequently with a wooden spoon, until thick, about 30 minutes. Stir in the herbs and salt to taste.

Lightly oil a loaf pan, and pour in the polenta. Cover and refrigerate; it will keep for up to a week.

When ready to grill or fry, unmold the polenta and cut it into ½-inch slices. Cut the slices into shapes if you like with a knife or large cookie cutters.

To grill, brush the polenta and the grill rack generously with olive oil. Grill the polenta until warmed through and nicely seared, 3 minutes per side.

To fry, brush the polenta and a heavy skillet or griddle generously with oil or butter. Over medium heat, fry the polenta until crisp and lightly browned, about 5 minutes per side.

. . . .

DO AHEAD: Cook and refrigerate the polenta.

IN THE MORNING (ABOUT 15 MINUTES): Cut and grill or fry the polenta.

. . . .

CILANTRO-LIME FRY BREAD WITH AVOCADO-CORN RELISH

Every summer, one of the largest Native American powwows in the United States is held about four blocks from my house on sacred soil that just happens to be Stanford University. From my bedroom window, I hear the drumming and chanting well into the night. During the day, my son and I go to the powwow to eat our yearly fill of fry bread. Traditionally, it is topped with honey or a generous amount of chili or tomato salsa. I came up with this Avocado Corn Relish using what I had acquired at the farmer's market one Saturday morning. The dough keeps in the refrigerator for 3 or 4 days. I pulled some out one morning when I was looking for a way to fill up a handful of my teenage son's friends. I served it next to eggs, and the boys decided they might never want toast again.

12 appetizer servings or 6 main-dish servings

2 CUPS UNBLEACHED WHITE FLOUR

1 CUP WHOLE WHEAT FLOUR

2½ TEASPOONS BAKING POWDER

1½ TEASPOONS SALT

1 TEASPOON CAYENNE (OPTIONAL)

1½ CUPS FINELY CHOPPED CILANTRO

GRATED ZEST OF 2 LIMES

1½ CUPS WARM WATER

ABOUT 2 CUPS VEGETABLE OIL

AVOCADO-CORN RELISH (RECIPE FOLLOWS)

Combine the flours, baking powder, salt, and cayenne in a medium-size bowl. Stir in the cilantro and lime zest. Gradually add the water, using your hands to blend it in. Knead the dough on a floured surface until smooth, about 5 minutes. Wipe out the bowl, coat the inside with oil, put the dough back in it, and set it aside, covered, for 30 minutes. (This is a good time to make the relish.)

Heat the 2 cups oil in a deep, heavy saucepan over medium-high heat. It's ready to use when a bit of dough dropped into it sizzles and rises to the top.

Divide the dough into twelve pieces, and pat each one into an oval about ⅛ inch thick. Fry the breads one or two at a time, turning, until lightly browned, about 2 minutes on each side. Drain on paper towels.

Serve hot topped with a generous portion of relish.

AVOCADO-CORN RELISH

Makes about 3 cups

1 FRESH EAR SWEET CORN, COOKED AND
   CHILLED
1 MEDIUM AVOCADO, PEELED, SEEDED, AND
   COARSELY CHOPPED
GRATED ZEST OF 1 LIME
JUICE OF 1 LIME
½ SMALL GREEN ONION, CHOPPED FINE
½ RED BELL PEPPER, CHOPPED FINE
1 TEASPOON GROUND CUMIN
½ CUP CHOPPED CILANTRO
CAYENNE OR CHOPPED HOT CHILE PEPPERS
   (OPTIONAL)
SALT

Cut the kernels from the corn cob. Toss them
in a medium-size bowl with the avocado, lime zest,
lime juice, onion, bell pepper, cumin, cilantro,
cayenne, and salt to taste. Cover and refrigerate.

....

DO AHEAD: Make the bread dough, and let it rest,
covered, in the refrigerator overnight. Prepare and
combine all the relish ingredients except the
avocado.

IN THE MORNING (ABOUT 20 MINUTES): Peel,
seed, and chop the avocado. Add it to the relish,
and adjust the seasonings. Fry the bread.

....

TAMARI POTATOES

This addictive dish has its roots in my hippie
days, when I used tamari instead of salt on everything.

4 servings

1½ POUNDS RED-SKINNED POTATOES,
   SCRUBBED
2 TABLESPOONS VEGETABLE OIL
1 MEDIUM ONION, CHOPPED
3 OR MORE TABLESPOONS TAMARI

Cut the potatoes into ½-inch chunks. Steam
them over boiling water for about 10 minutes,
until tender.

Heat a heavy skillet over medium-high
heat, and add the oil. When it's hot, sauté the
potatoes and onion, turning, until they are well
browned and crispy, 6 to 8 minutes.

Remove the pan from the heat, and sprinkle
tamari over all. Taste and add more if you like.
Serve immediately.

....

DO AHEAD: Cut and steam the potatoes and
chop the onion. Refrigerate, covered.

IN THE MORNING (ABOUT 10 MINUTES): Fry
and season the potatoes and onions as directed.

....

SWEET POTATO HOME FRIES

Serve this slightly sweet version of down-home potatoes with ham and eggs and hand-cut slices of whole wheat toast spread thick with fruit butter. It's a great way to use up extra baked sweet potatoes. If using bacon fat, crumble the fried bacon and add it to the potatoes at the end.

2 to 4 servings

½ MEDIUM ONION

2 MEDIUM SWEET POTATOES, BAKED UNTIL
   STILL FIRM AT THE CENTER

3 TABLESPOONS BACON FAT, BUTTER, OR
   VEGETABLE OIL

SALT AND FRESHLY GROUND PEPPER

Chop the onion and potatoes into ½-inch pieces.

Heat the fat in a heavy skillet over medium heat. Sauté the onion until slightly soft, about 3 minutes. Add the potatoes and cook, tossing frequently, until the vegetables are slightly browned all over, about 5 minutes. Season to taste with salt and pepper. Serve hot.

....

DO AHEAD: Bake and cut up the sweet potatoes, chop the onion, and refrigerate, covered.

IN THE MORNING (ABOUT 15 MINUTES): Fry the vegetables as directed.

....

POTATOES, PEPPERS, AND MUSHROOMS

Offer this earthy combination with eggs, or top individual portions with thick slices of tomato and mozzarella cheese for a hearty, one-dish breakfast.

2 main-dish servings or 4 side-dish servings

2 TABLESPOONS OLIVE OIL

1 MEDIUM ONION, COARSELY CHOPPED

1 LARGE OR 2 SMALL POTATOES, SCRUBBED
   AND THINLY SLICED

1 LARGE GREEN OR RED BELL PEPPER, SEEDED
   AND COARSELY CHOPPED

¼ POUND MUSHROOMS, THICKLY SLICED

2 GARLIC CLOVES, CRUSHED

1 TABLESPOON CHOPPED FRESH OREGANO

SALT AND FRESHLY GROUND PEPPER

Heat a large skillet over medium-low heat and add the oil. Sauté the onion and potatoes for about 10 minutes. Stir in the bell pepper, mushrooms, garlic, and oregano. Cook, turning often, until the potatoes are soft, 15 to 20 minutes. Season to taste with salt and pepper.

....

DO AHEAD: Cut up all the vegetables, crush garlic, and chop oregano. Refrigerate all, covered.

IN THE MORNING (ABOUT 30 MINUTES): Cook the dish as directed.

....

POTATO-ZUCCHINI HASH BROWNS

Grating zucchini and yellow summer squash in with the potatoes gives these hash browns a harlequin-like appearance. Around my house, eggs are often forgotten when I fry up a pan of hash browns. They're a welcome way to start a summer day, especially when topped with bits of ripe, juicy tomato.

4 servings

1½ POUNDS ZUCCHINI AND/OR YELLOW SUMMER SQUASH

1½ POUNDS BAKING POTATOES, SCRUBBED

1 MEDIUM ONION

1 TEASPOON SALT

FRESHLY GROUND PEPPER

3 TABLESPOONS VEGETABLE OIL

CHOPPED TOMATO AND FRESH HERBS FOR GARNISH

Coarsely grate the zucchini, potato, and onion. Mix thoroughly with the salt and set in a colander over the sink for 10 minutes, pressing occasionally to squeeze out the water. Season to taste with pepper.

Heat a heavy, 10-inch skillet over medium heat, and add the oil. When it's hot, add the vegetable mixture and press it down firmly with a spatula. Turn the heat to medium-low and cook until golden brown on one side, about 10 minutes.

If you can, flip the whole thing over; if not, cut it into wedges and turn. Cook, uncovered, until brown on the other side, 6 or 8 minutes more.

Transfer to plates and serve immediately garnished with tomato and herbs.

....

DO AHEAD: Grate and drain the zucchini, potatoes, and onion; season with pepper. Chop tomato and herbs. Refrigerate all, covered.

IN THE MORNING (ABOUT 20 MINUTES): Cook the dish as directed.

....

SCALLOPED POTATOES

It seems I can never make enough scalloped potatoes. My family loves them at any meal, but especially breakfast. These are similar to Potatoes Dauphinoise except that flour rather than heavy cream holds them together. These are great made with sweet potatoes, too.

4 servings with leftovers

**3 POUNDS POTATOES, SCRUBBED AND
 SLICED THIN**

1 MEDIUM-LARGE YELLOW ONION, SLICED THIN

ABOUT ¼ CUP FLOUR

**ABOUT ¼ CUP BUTTER (OPTIONAL, BUT
 DELICIOUS)**

SALT AND FRESHLY GROUND PEPPER

MILK OR HALF AND HALF

6 OUNCES GRATED CHEDDAR CHEESE

Preheat the oven to 375 degrees.

Spread thin layers of potatoes and onions in a 2-quart or 2½-quart casserole that's about 3 inches deep. Dust each layer generously with flour, dab it with butter, and sprinkle it with salt and pepper. End with a layer of potatoes, and sprinkle it with salt and pepper but not flour. Pour in enough milk to reach about 1 inch below the top.

Bake for about 45 minutes, until the potatoes are very tender when pierced with a fork. Turn up the heat to 450 degrees and remove the casserole from the oven. Sprinkle it with the Cheddar and return it to the oven until the cheese melts, about 5 minutes.

. . . .

DO AHEAD: Prepare and bake the potatoes.

IN THE MORNING (5 TO 15 MINUTES): Cut the potatoes into serving-size squares and reheat in a microwave for 5 minutes or a 375-degree oven, until warm throughout.

. . . .

REAL CORNED BEEF HASH

Serve poached or fried eggs over this crisp, chunky hash, so that when the golden yolks are pierced they meld with its saltiness.

2 to 4 servings

1 POUND BAKING POTATOES, SCRUBBED

1 MEDIUM ONION

8 TO 12 OUNCES CORNED BEEF

2 TABLESPOONS VEGETABLE OIL

SALT AND FRESHLY GROUND PEPPER

Chop the potatoes, onion, and corned beef into even bite-size pieces, about ½-inch cubes.

Heat a 10-inch skillet over medium heat, and add the oil. When it's hot, sauté the potato, onion, and corned beef, turning the mixture with a spatula, until the potato is soft and all the ingredients are crispy and browned, about 10 minutes. Season to taste with salt and pepper.

. . . .

DO AHEAD: Chop the potatoes and onion, and sauté until the onions are soft, about 5 minutes. Chop the corned beef. Refrigerate all, covered.

IN THE MORNING (ABOUT 15 MINUTES): Rewarm the potatoes and onion, add the corned beef, and cook until warmed through and browned. Season with salt and pepper.

. . . .

TARRAGON SEAFOOD HASH

2 servings

¾ POUND FRESH FISH OR SHELLFISH

1 TABLESPOON VEGETABLE OIL

2 TABLESPOONS CHOPPED RED ONION

¼ CUP COARSELY CHOPPED RED BELL PEPPER

2 GARLIC CLOVES, MINCED

½ CUP CUBED COOKED POTATOES

2 TABLESPOONS CRISP DRY WHITE WINE

½ TO ¾ CUP CLAM JUICE OR FISH STOCK

1 TO 2 TABLESPOONS CHOPPED FRESH
   TARRAGON

1 TO 2 TABLESPOONS CHOPPED FRESH PARSLEY

SALT AND FRESHLY GROUND PEPPER

Wash and shell the shellfish. Rinse the fish fillets and cut them into bite-size pieces. Cover and refrigerate.

Heat the oil in a 10-inch skillet over medium heat. Sauté the onion, bell pepper, and garlic until soft, about 5 minutes. Add the potatoes and cook, stirring, until warmed through and slightly browned, about 5 minutes. Add the wine, clam juice, tarragon, and parsley. Bring it to a simmer, and add the seafood. Cover and cook until the fish is flaky and the shellfish is cooked through, about 5 minutes. Season with salt and pepper to taste.

DO AHEAD: Clean and cut up the seafood. Prepare and cook the vegetable mixture. Refrigerate, covered.

IN THE MORNING (ABOUT 15 MINUTES): Rewarm the vegetables and proceed as directed.

PIPERADE

This dish is wonderful served with grilled polenta, eggs, grilled bread, or spicy Italian sausage.

4 servings

1 SMALL YELLOW ONION

1 MEDIUM RED OR GREEN BELL PEPPER, SEEDED

3 MEDIUM TOMATOES, SEEDED

1 TABLESPOON LIGHT OLIVE OIL

2 OR MORE TABLESPOONS CHOPPED FRESH
   OREGANO, BASIL, AND/OR THYME

1 OR 2 GARLIC CLOVES, MINCED

SALT AND FRESHLY GROUND PEPPER

Coarsely chop the onion, pepper, and tomatoes.

Heat a 10-inch skillet over medium heat, and add the oil. Sauté the onion and pepper until soft, about 5 minutes. Stir in the tomatoes, herbs, and garlic, and cook just until hot, about 5 minutes. Season with salt and pepper.

DO AHEAD: Cut up all the ingredients and refrigerate, covered.

IN THE MORNING (15 MINUTES): Cook as directed.

Menu Suggestions

A BREAKFAST AFTER CAMPING AT THE BEACH

Hearty, flavorful, uncomplicated yet interesting, most can be done beforehand and taken in a cooler to be assembled or cooked that morning. Fried Pasta and Eggs with Green Onions, Garlic, and Asiago Cheese are a great way to use up last night's leftover spaghetti and fill hikers with carbohydrates to keep them going most of the day.

Fried Pasta and Eggs with Green Onions, Garlic, and Asiago Cheese (page 33)
Piperade (page 111)
Bacon, Cheddar, and Parsley Soda Bread (page 98)
Tamari Potatoes (page 106)

BREAKFAST ON THE DECK

Pull your mattress or futon out onto the deck for a night of dreaming under the stars, and present this feast the next morning.

Hominy Grits with Peppers, Cajun Shrimp, and Basted Eggs (page 61)
Sage and Onion Pita Bread (page 99)
Fresh oranges and berries with mint

A HOT SUMMER NIGHT'S TEENAGE SLUMBER PARTY

Breakfast Burritos (page 30)
Josh's Chilaquiles with Avocado (page 26)
Fresh Corn and Bacon Pudding (page 58)
Fruit Pizzas (page 18)

BREAKFAST OF ELEGANCE

Mimosas
Melon with Prosciutto, Mint, and Champagne (page 11)
Buckwheat-Herb Blinis with Caviar, Sour Cream, and Chive Blossoms (page 71)
Crab Cakes in Chive Custard (page 35)

BREAKFAST AFTER THE NEW YEAR'S EVE PARTY

A bone-sticking meal for hungry revelers.

Winter Squash Pancakes (page 70)
Bacon, Cheddar, Chard, Leek, and Chutney Omelet (page 43)
Maple-Baked Pears with Aged Cheddar (page 13)
Hominy–Red Onion Bread with Chipotle Butter (page 97)

BREAKFAST FOR DINNER

For those evenings when you want to crawl back into bed and eat that hearty breakfast you didn't have time for in the morning.

Whole Wheat Sage Waffles with Shiitake
    Mushroom Gravy (page 79)
Apple, Ham, Sage Derby, and Chive Frittata
    (page 50)
Sweet Potato Home Fries (page 107)
Smoked pork chops

Polenta with Maple Syrup and Mascarpone
    (page 60)

BREAKFAST FOR A SICK
LOVED ONE

My Mom's Nurturing Mashed Soft-Cooked
    Eggs (page 25)
Chicken Broth with Toasted Bread and Italian
    Cheese (page 54)
Toast with Quick Fruit Butters (page 6)

BREAKFAST IN THE HAMMOCK

When I was a kid, my favorite place to be was in the big green hammock in our backyard. I would drag out a sheet and pillow and take naps, sleep out overnight, secretly meet boyfriends, read books, do homework, daydream, and eat any meal my mom would permit beneath the giant oak tree in that big green hammock.

Jonah's Egg-in-the-Eye over Ratatouille (page 27)
Sweet Potato Home Fries (page 107)
Savory Muffins (page 92)

COMFORTING RICE WITH MILK, SUGAR, AND BUTTER (PAGE 55)

BREAKFAST ON VALENTINE'S DAY

Romantic and feminine; use a heart-shaped cutter for the biscuits.

Sour Cream, Orange, and Lavender Biscuits (page 85)

Blintzes with Berries (page 15)

Potato-Onion Nests with Creamed Spinach and Eggs (page 36)

BREAKFAST FROM A CHILD FOR MOM OR DAD OR GRANDPARENTS

These dishes can be made by an older child with a little adult help.

Bacon, Cheddar, Chard, Leek, and Chutney Omelet (page 43)

Cinnamon–Brown Sugar Drop Biscuits (page 84)

Tamari Potatoes (page 106)

BREAKFAST FOR A NEW LOVER

Crab Cakes in Chive Custard (page 35)

Baguette with Cambozola Brie, Chives, and Strawberries (page 8)

Buckwheat-Herb Blinis with Caviar, Sour Cream, and Chive Blossoms (page 71)

BREAKFAST FOR ONE

To nurture yourself in bed.

Fresh Fruit Omelet (page 14)

Comforting Rice with Milk, Sugar, and Butter (page 55)

CHRISTMAS DAY BREAKFAST

Buttermilk-Pecan Waffles (page 77)

Smoked Salmon, Avocado, Cheddar, and Green Onion Omelet (page 39)

BEFORE THE FEAST ON THANKSGIVING DAY

Scrambled Eggs on Caramelized Onions (page 31)

Winter Fruit Compote with No-Bake Orange-Almond Oat Cakes (page 16)

INDEX